S0-ADF-290

The Catholic
Theological Union
LIBRARY
Chicago, Ill.

WITHDRAWN

160

The Lawyer Looks Beyond the Law

Essays in Human Dignity

Issued by the
WILLIAM J. KERBY FOUNDATION

The Catholic
Theological Union
LIBRARY
Chicago, Ill.

THE CATHOLIC UNIVERSITY OF AMERICA PRESS
WASHINGTON 17, D. C.
1951

Copyright 1951 by

THE CATHOLIC UNIVERSITY OF AMERICA PRESS, INC.

Manufactured by
Universal Lithographers, Inc.
Baltimore 2, Md.
U.S.A.

Contents

Foreword

This volume includes the lectures which were presented at the Twelfth Annual Sunday Morning Religious Round Table Conferences, sponsored by the School of Law, under the direction of the Department of Religious Education of The Catholic University of America. These lectures were delivered in 1951 by specialists in the field of American and religious thought. The purpose of the lectures was primarily to provide a concise and interesting explanation of the application of basic truths to the problems of today, especially for lawyers and law students, both Catholic and non-Catholic.

In these essays the reader is invited to look beyond the Law. The leader of each Round Table has sought to communicate, in a single lecture, the significant factors in subject matter which would otherwise require weeks, or even months, of study and investigation for adequate understanding.

Publication of the lectures was made possible by the generosity of the Kerby Foundation.

Dr. Brendan F. Brown, Dean
School of Law
The Catholic University of America

The Lawyer and Scripture

REV. GERARD S. SLOYAN, Ph. D.
Instructor in Religious Education
The Catholic University of America

In tiny St. John's Episcopal Church in Richmond, Virginia, on March 23, 1775, where the Richmond Convention was in heated session to discuss the oppressive encroachments of the British Crown, Patrick Henry addressed to the delegates a series of pointed questions that rose in dramatic crescendo:

> Are we disposed 'to be of the number of those who, having eyes, see not, and having ears, hear not, the things which so nearly concern their temporal salvation? For my part . . . I am willing to know the whole truth; to know the worst and to provide for it. I have but one lamp by which my feet are guided, and that is the lamp of experience. I know of no way of judging of the future but by the past.

Then, after a devastating summary of British breaches of good faith and peaceful intent, he went on:

> If we wish to be free . . . we must fight! . . . An appeal to arms and to the God of Hosts is all that is left us . . . We shall not fight our battles alone. There is a just God who presides over the destinies of nations, and who will raise up friends to fight our battles for us . . .
> It is vain, sir, to extenuate the matter. The gentlemen may cry, Peace, peace!—but there is no peace. The war is actually begun! . . . Our brethren are already in the field! Why stand we here idle? . . . Is life so dear, or peace so sweet, as to be purchased at the price of chains or slavery? Forbid it, Almighty God![1]

Now, that is a truncated version of a famous speech, and the principle of selection was this: that most of the phrases singled out had about them the authorship of God the Holy Ghost, speaking through David the King, Isaias the Prophet, and Christ the Priest, before ever they were forged by Mr. Patrick Henry of Virginia. There is a nobility in his words

---

[1] William Wirt, *Sketches of the Life and Character of Patrick Henry*, Philadelphia, 1817, in Henry Steele Commager and Allan Nevins, *The Heritage of America* (Boston: Little, Brown, 1951), pp. 140-42.

deriving not simply from the justice of his cause or his not inconsiderable skill as a rhetorician, but from the fact that they have God as their first author, and what he says is said well. More than that, the common coin of Scripture among the Richmond delegates was the sign of a commonly held religious conviction. It is logical and reasonable to speak in words inspired by God only when you believe that he is, and can do the works claimed for him. Otherwise it is a disgusting sham. Early Americans largely believed in such a Being of infinite power. They believed that he had transmitted to them his own thoughts, preserved in a book. There was, therefore, neither hypocrisy nor political bombast in the public invocation of his name and his writings by the greater number.

Concerning the point just made, this much must be clearly understood. Of all the reasons that can be advanced for the reading and use of Holy Scripture, undoubtedly the least worthy of consideration is the one that sees in it a tool for the advancement of human ends. If you have ever been repelled by the notion that the Bible is a treasure-house of phrase-making and imagery, to be rifled by men in turning out their puny speeches and summaries, their novels and essays, be assured that you will encounter no such idea in these lines. There is something particularly sacrilegious or at least saddening in the spectacle of your literary man or your jurist reading the Bible day after day searching for everything there but faith. You pick up a magazine or book-review supplement and are surprised to learn that some consistently unbelieving or skeptical person is thoroughly conversant with what to him is the purely human literature of the Hebrews and the followers of the man Jesus. It is his model in psychology, narrative form, description, everything but religion. H. L. Mencken is such a person. So were Shelley, A. E. Housman, Thomas Wolfe, Edna Millay. Their number is legion, their Bible knowledge enviable.

There are few engaged in the teaching of literature so brave or so foolhardy as to minimize the power and influence of the Bible. College and university courses extol the flavor of the Hebrew and Greek originals and the beauty of the King James, commonly called the Authorized, Version. To illustrate, attend briefly to the Oriental imagery

2

of the Psalms: "The sea beheld and fled; Jordan turned back. The mountains skipped like rams, the hills like the lambs of the flock." (Ps. 113, 3) "I am like water poured out . . . My heart has become like wax . . . My throat is dried up like baked clay, my tongue cleaves to my jaws." (Ps. 21, 15f.) "Though I am shrivelled like a leathern flask in the smoke, I have not forgotten your statutes." (Ps. 118, 83)[2] But often the praise of literary men is lavished on an empty shell, for they are hardly done admitting the Bible's profound effect on thought and language before they are engaged in describing it as a fabric of myths and empty dreams, of bad history, worse science, and bloody deeds masked by a religiosity that is little better than the pagan cults from which it sprung. They say that Christ was a deceiver, the Resurrection a fraud, and St. Paul the author of Christianity as a doctrinal system, and in the same breath they speak of the simple beauty of the parables, the unrivaled account of the love of David and Jonathan, the rustic idyll that is the story of Ruth. A professor of English literature has been quoted in this vein, saying in extension of Oscar Wilde's epigram: "The only bad book is the poorly written one. Style is everything. Subject matter means nothing. Look at the Bible."

Well, let us look at the Bible briefly, in the hope that it will convince us we do not look at it half enough. Let us see what this library of seventy-two books, composed over a 1400 or 1500 year span (roughly between 1350 B. C. and 100 A. D.), has to offer the Christian man whose trade happens to be the promotion of justice. Presuming on, rather than troubling to demonstrate, our common view of the matter, we say that the God and Father of us all has, through his Spirit, given knowledge of his Son by means of promise and fulfillment, of preparation and consummation. We believe that the Lord first cultivated a people who would be a worthy root and stock of the long-awaited Vine of Deliverance, the man Jesus Christ, and that the record of his doings and those of his Son has been preserved in writing. It was not simply that men recorded what they had observed. The Bible was not composed in that way. God entered into their minds and impelled them to write those

<hr>

[2] The Episcopal Committee of the Confraternity of Christian Doctrine, *The book of Psalms,* tr. from the Hebrew, (Paterson: St. Anthony Guild, 1950).

3

things, and only those things, that would serve his purpose best. He did not treat them as puppets or automatons. They retained their defects of character often, their limited powers of observation, their peculiar literary weaknesses or strengths. Yet by divine power, the written product that emerged was totally the work of God and totally the work of Moses; the diction no less of the Holy Spirit than of Jeremias, John, or Jude. This breathing of the Holy Spirit, this guidance of the human mind and will resulting in divine-human authorship is known as inspiration. Testimony to the inspired Scriptures is found within the books themselves. There is no lapse in logic in asking God what manner of gift precisely, he has given us in transmitting the written corpus. St. Paul's is the human voice that provides the answer:

> God's word to us is something alive, full of energy; it can penetrate deeper than any two-edged sword, reaching the very division between soul and spirit, between joints and marrow, quick to distinguish every thought and design in our hearts. (Heb. 4, 12)

Testimony to the inspired character of the Scriptures is something that is sought ultimately from the Church. A median process is to use New Testament writings simply as works of reliable history in order to establish what the faith of the Church regarding the Hebrew Scriptures was.

The Bible is not a "dead book" as Catholic expositors sometimes unhappily claim in their efforts to contrast it with a living Church. No, it is a living book in a living Church, God speaking through his prophets, his Son, his friends, in a way that the living Church is empowered to understand most readily and best. "My words are spirit and life," Christ said (Jn. 6, 64), and he meant precisely that. Dull nature resists sanctification, rebels at being lifted above itself. Theological propositions and moral demands can fall upon the ears of the natural man with one effect, and that a soporific. Then God speaks:

"I am God Almighty; live as in my sight and be perfect." (Gen. 17, 1) "I, thy God, the Lord Almighty, am jealous in my love; be my enemy, and thy children, to the third and fourth generations, shall make amends; love me, keep my commandments, and mercy shall be thine a thousand-fold." (Deut. 5, 9f.) "Your own eyes have witnessed how the

4

Lord your God carried you through the desert as a man carries his little son, all the long road you have travelled to reach this spot." (Deut. 1, 31) "And with that, the king went up to the room over the gate in bitter sorrow, and wept there. 'O, my son Absalom', he said as he went, 'my son, my son Absalom! Would to God I had died instead of thee, my son, my son!' " (II Kings, 18, 33) "Did Sion complain, 'The Lord has forsaken me, my own Master gives me never a thought?' What, can a woman forget her child that is still unweaned, pity no longer the son she bore in her womb? Let her forget; I will not be forgetful of thee." (Is. 49, 14ff.) "Sprinkle me with a wand of hyssop, and I shall be clean; washed, I shall be whiter than snow; tidings send me of good news and rejoicing, and the body that lies in the dust shall thrill with pride." (Ps. 50, 9f.) "Do not be afraid, my little flock. Your Father has determined to give you his Kingdom. Sell what you have and give alms . . . where your treasure-house is, there your heart is too." (Luke 12, 32ff.) "Jesus said to him, 'My friend, on what errand hast thou come?' Then they came forward, and laid their hands on Jesus, and held him fast." (Mt. 26, 50) "Everyone who believes that Jesus is the Christ is a child of God, and to love the parent is to love his child . . . Loving God means keeping his commandments, and these commandments of his are not a burden to us." (I Jn. 5, 1 and 3) "I am Alpha, I am Omega, I am before all, I am at the end of all, the beginning of all things and their end." (Apoc. 22, 13)[3]

Those are the words that have the power to pierce the human marrow, to test the spirit of man and see what is in him. It is not revealed that a catechism can do that, or a preacher discoursing lucidly on Christian apologetics, or a Catholic press, however well turned out. It *is* revealed that the Bible, wherein God speaks to men direct, can cut like a blade of Damascus. "Everything in the scripture has been divinely inspired, and has its uses; to instruct us, to expose our errors, to correct our faults, to educate us in holy living; so God's servant will become a master of his craft, and each noble task that comes will find him ready for it." (II Tim. 3, 10f.)

---

[3] All Knox translation. The same is used in the two quotations that conclude the essay, while the remainder are from the Douay-Rheims version.

Masters of your craft! That is the goal. Defenders of the right, protagonists of God-inspired right order, enemies of deceit, of lying and cheating for gain. So it is to be a lawyer. It is much the same to be a Christian man: indeed, to be the one is the better part of being the other. Seize the means of holiness and justice held out to you in the reading of the Scriptures, and the integrity and wisdom that you know your profession requires in you will be more than within your grasp.

There are in Christian life two spiritual foods that should never be taken separately; one is the Bread of the Eucharist, and the other is the Bread of the Word of God in the Scriptures.[4] The two go side by side. They are of equal importance. At one time the Book of Gospels was kept in the tabernacle, just as today it is incensed at High Mass. In the Mass, theoretically we receive both nourishments together, in accord with the Church's ancient plan. Actually, Scripture-knowledge, which is Christ-knowledge, often runs sadly behind Christ-reception, and the result can be a type of superstition in which the Body of Christ is used as a kind of charm or talisman. The true effect of the Eucharist consists in acts of love, that is what sacramental union with Christ is meant to achieve, and unless a man's mind and heart have been turned to God and instructed by his word, he will be unresponsive, dull, cold. There are communicants in America by the hundreds of thousands: annually, monthly, weekly. There are tepid men, men uncharitable toward neighbors, ill-tempered, selfish, arrested in spiritual development, sharp in business dealings, and many are the same hundreds of thousands. How can a person go on so, energetic in all Catholic matters and yet unshaken by the Gift of Wisdom, insensible to the deeper spiritual realities in the persons and events around? Well, he may know but never realize, he may have Christ as his barely sufficient Companion in the dark because Christ the Light has never flooded the obscure places in his mind and heart. It is the Lamp of the Word that does that. A lamp disguised as the thick, black, tab-edged, formidable, unread volume in your house called the Bible.

[4] The thought of Conrad Pepler, O.P., is reflected throughout this paragraph. Cf. "The Bread of the Word," *Orate Fratres,* May 18, 1947, pp. 307-11. Reprinted from *Blackfriars,* XXVII, No. 316.

One would be unwise to make that generalization carelessly. It is not universally true. Some of you, I have no doubt, are consistent readers of the New Testament at least, and some possibly, of both Testaments. I who presume to exhort you am from a family where the Bible was not traditionally read. Introduction through the school assignments of the children was its mode of entry into an otherwise faithful Catholic home. The reason for the Catholic lag in delighting in our own heritage is known to most of you. Heresies surrounding the Word and the Book have made us unaccustomed to reading the Scriptures. It, instead of Peter, became the rock on which all sorts of churches have been built. But whilst the heresies brought about a certain de-emphasis in Bible use among Catholics, they did it indirectly. I mean by that that there was never in the Church any official discouragement of Bible reading, as such, which is of course quite another thing from the anathemas published in England and elsewhere against vernacular translations which were all of them tendentious or heretical. The early Protestants made the Book the symbol of their doctrine, a thing as arbitrary in them as it was foolish in us to let transpire. "We have no Mass, no incense and trumpery, no Jesuitical theologizing, we have the word of God, living and energizing," said the heretics of four hundred years, just as of ten minutes, ago. And the Catholic answer, instead of a vehement, "No, by George, you shall not appropriate the Book Christ gave his Church!"; was either a default of response, or a lame defense that spoke optimistically of the *equivalent* use of Scripture in the Mass, in prayer books, and in books of doctrine.

Ask any Catholic student to account for the present-day non-use of the Bible among members of the Church that claims it for her own, and he will tell you of the dangers of private interpretation, "wresting the Scriptures to one's own destruction," (if only he were familiar with the phrase). But that is not the real reason, it is a post-factum rationalization. Catholics do not read the Bible because they are victims of a bad and reprehensible tradition of not reading the Bible! Why, for every papal pronouncement and exhortation on frequent Communion in the fifty years of this century there has been one insisting on the need for the Scriptures as the daily food of Catholics. But the response

7

to this latter call has been slower, and the danger of a one-sided sacramentalism has begun to appear. Seldom has a Christian people been as widely and potentially well instructed in their faith as in our country and time. Hundreds of thousands are being trained in schools, even past the college level, conducted by the Church. Her priests are readily accessible should theological or other difficulties arise out of Scripture reading. They are not universal scholars, but can deal readily with ordinary uncertainties. Heresy is not in the air, excepting indifferentism and materialism, and the Bible is the mortal enemy of both. "All you that thirst, come to the waters: and you that have no money, make haste, buy and eat: come ye, buy wine and milk without money, and without any price." (Is. 55, 1) So says our Heavenly Father as he proffers the meat and drink of his inspired word.

Aside from the fact that this is God's second most direct method of speaking to his people (preceded only by the verbal revelations themselves recounted in Scripture), there is about Bible reading the particular efficacy that in it dogmas come to life. One does not struggle through abstract propositions; one walks with God and talks with him, sees him at work, now merciful, now just, ever loving. One's whole being is reached, intellect, will, imagination, emotions. David sins and lives to repent deeply; Tobias braves the loss of everything he owns out of reverence for the dead; Jezabel falls to the dogs who lick away her painted smile; Philip grows weary of faith and asks for sight of the Father; Christ weeps for his dead friend and people say, "See how he loved him." These things touch us men because they have to do with men. God lives in his servants, even in his adversaries, but most especially does he live in his Incarnate Son. He does not speak to human hearts in a series of proof-texts. His living word is not handed out piecemeal. The form assumed in certain uses of the Scriptures—quotes, then two lines, quotes closed, and in parenthesis, "Galatians, 5, 26," or whatever it might be—is not the form in which God hopes to stir men to belief and action. He employs narrative, suspense, love poetry, prophetic warning, reasoned argument (as in Christ's discourses and St. Paul's epistles), parable, character portrayal.

Where can you learn of the slow and certain progress

from unhealthy curiosity to temptation to sin so well as in the third chapter of Genesis? Who informs you better on the downfall of the crafty in the working out of God's justice than the Book of Esther? From what purer source can you drink in the doctrines of divine love, trust in God, firm adherence to his revelation, than from the lips of Christ his Son? You will learn things you had not known before, granted. The incompleteness of God's revelation on doctrinal and moral matters 3,000 years ago may disturb you. The freedom with which the evangelists report Christ's words and deeds, omitting or including details as suits their immediate purpose best, may cause a revision in your erroneously held concept of what inspiration and inerrancy properly consist in. Well enough. God will give the grace of understanding upon inquiry, so delighted will he be that you are reading his masterwork. Instruction will come, as Paul promises; your errors will be exposed, your faults gradually corrected, and there will be a slow but clearly observable progress in holy living.

The lawyer has a special stake in Holy Writ, as I need hardly tell you. So much of the earliest inspired Scriptures was concerned with legal prescriptions—liturgical, hygienic, political, proprietary—that the Mosaic writings, and in a looser sense even the whole Old Testament, are referred to simply as *Ha Torah,* the Law. The entire apostolic argument to the Jews on why they were bound by God to accept Jesus as the Christ is based on the temporary binding force of his solemn contract with them—on its termination, previously agreed upon, when certain conditions should have been fulfilled. St. Paul, born Saul in the city of Tarsus, made the admirable theologian that he did because of his careful training in the Law, for the Jew a thing civil and religious alike. He boasted of his training under the master Gamaliel, just as a contemporary American would claim academic kinship with Dean Pound, Justice Holmes, or Justice Frankfurter. You will find Paul praising Christ again and again for his grace and love, so vastly superior to the Law. Not that he had lost his sense of justice was this the case, but because he saw the human condition to be such that only an outpouring of love and mercy could rescue man from the consequences of his strict deserts under the Mosaic code.

9

Coming to later Christian times, though still very early in the Church's life—the 4th century—there is the case of the imperial governor in northern Italy, Ambrose, schooled in the law, and in his thirty-fifth year a still unbaptized catechumen in accord with the abuse prevalent at the time. He attended a diocesan synod as governor to keep order in the election of a new bishop, and so great was his reputation as a fair-minded legist that he was unexpectedly chosen for the Church office by acclaim. "Let daily reading (of the Scriptures) be our practice," he later wrote, "in such a way that we will be disposed to imitate those things we meditate upon." (Exp. in Ps. 118, *Sermo Duodecimus*) St. John Chrysostom had some excellent advice for the laymen among his fourth-century flock. "Not only monks stand in need of the Scriptures," he said. "Every man suffers daily wounds, and word from the divine Scriptures does more than fire to soften the hardened soul." (*Hom. in Matt.* II, 10) "To neglect them is to subject oneself to poverty and to potential harm." (*Ibid., Hom.* XLVII, 3) "They are a mirror that not only reflects deformity but can also transform it into surpassing beauty, given human willingness." (*Ibid., Hom.* IV 8) Do you like that idea of a mirror of truth that flatters no one, misleads no one? St. Yves, 13th century patron of lawyers, frequently gave conferences to adults on the Scriptures, but the true measure of his mastery of Holy Writ was that the little children used to follow him through the streets to hear him tell stories about Christ.[5] That should be goal enough for any lawyer-father to aim at with his own children.

St. Thomas More, Lord Chancellor of England, used to have one of his daughters read a passage from the Bible at meals in the home as is done in religious houses, then a short commentary, followed by family discussion. On Good Friday all in his household would gather to hear the Passion read. He pleaded in the 1520's for an authorized Catholic translation of the Scriptures into English but none came except for the snatches that he rendered in his own books of devotion. Meanwhile the reformers Tyndale and Coverdale, Taverner and "Matthew" were flooding the country with their tendentious translations. More's last plea of de-

---

[5] For this and the foregoing citations, cf. William H. Russell, *The Bible and Character* (Philadelphia: Dolphin Press, 1934), Chap. I, *passim,* and p. 85.

fence in court was based on his conception of the necessary continuity of England as a member of the body of Christendom:

> For, as St. Paul said of the Corinthians, "I have regenerated you, my children in Christ"; so might St. Gregory, Pope of Rome, of whom, by St. Augustine his messenger, we first received the Christian faith, of us English men, truly say: "You are my children, because I have given to you everlasting salvation."[6]

It was to no avail. After condemnation, his final word in court was his hope that like St. Stephen and St. Paul, he and his judges would " . . . hereafter in Heaven, meet merrily all together, to our everlasting salvation." More wrote beautiful meditations on Christ's Passion while in captivity, and died with the *Miserere*, the 50th Psalm, on his lips. But lest you think that his piety succeeded in swallowing up his professionalism, it will be good to learn that on his way to the gallows a woman along the way reviled him thus:

> "Do you remember, Master More, that when you were Chancellor you were my hard friend, and did me great injury in giving wrong judgment against me?" "Woman," (quoth he), "I am now going to my death. I remember well the whole matter; if now I were to give sentence again, I assure thee, I would not alter it. Thou hast no injury, so content thee, and trouble me not."[7]

So had his reading of Solomon, of St. Joseph the just man, and of Christ the Sun of Justice convinced him of the justice of his course.

It was a happier day in the world when public men could have recourse publicly to the idea of God, his words and his works, and expect to be understood as though they had spoken fact and not fancy. In 1765 Sir William Blackstone wrote in his *Commentaries on the Laws of England:* "To deny the possibility, nay the actual existence of witchcraft and sorcery is flatly to contradict the revealed word of God."[8] He was referring to the Book of Exodus (22:18), where under Mosaic law it is said that sorcerers, or traffickers with evil spirits, "must not be allowed to live." I do not quote with approval the misapplication of an ancient pre-

---

[6] R. W. Chambers, *Thomas More* (New York: Harcourt, Brace, 1935), p. 341.

[7] R. W. Chambers, *op. cit.,* p. 348.

[8] *Commentaries on the Laws of England,* ed. Thomas M. Cooley (Chicago: Callaghan & Co., 1899), Book IV, p. 60.

scription for a particular people made by British and American jurists to unfortunate women doubtfully under Satan's power. I simply point out the ease with which a man turned to divine sanction as authoritative, on a point which he considered indisputable, in his legal writing of two centuries ago.

It was a commonplace for America's patriots and leaders of another day to have been nourished by the Scriptures.[9] The same Patrick Henry cited above, hardly a notably religious man, nonetheless made a very good end. (It is good to know that lawyers occasionally get a chance to do that. They are so often identified with the setting in order of other men's houses.) In any case, just before his death he said of the Bible:

> Here is a book worth more than all others ever printed: yet it is my misfortune never to have read it with proper attention and feeling until lately. It is now too late. I trust in the mercy of God.[10]

Too late to read it perhaps, but he had mastered enough of the divine message to catch its spirit. "There is one thing more I wish I could give them," he said in his will, speaking of his family, "and that is the Christian religion. If they had that, and I had not given them one shilling they would be rich, and if they had not that, and I had given them all the world, they would be poor."[11]

Many an American military leader has sought solace and help from the Book of Books. You have doubtless heard of the piety of Thomas "Stonewall" Jackson—"Old Blue Light," as his men called him, and "Deacon Jackson." He was dead at thirty-nine, but the many hours he spent pondering on the things of God gave him a seriousness beyond his years. "Let our government acknowledge the God of the Bible as its God," he once wrote, "and we may expect soon to be a happy and independent people."[12] When Jackson spoke that way no one accused him of hypocrisy or of accomodating his habitual manner of thinking to the exi-

---

[9] For an interesting if frequently shallow "tracking down of the Bible's influence on English and American Life," cf. Lawrence E. Nelson, *Our Roving Bible* (Nashville: Abingdon-Cokesbury, 1945).

[10] George Stimpson, *A Book About History* (New York: Harper and Brothers, 1950), p. 112.

[11] *Loc. cit.*

[12] *Ibid.*, p. 322.

gencies of a public utterance. "It is from the heart's overflow that the mouth speaks; a good man utters good words from his store of goodness. . . . " (Mt. 12, 25)

When Abraham Lincoln said publicly that just as no city or house divided against itself could stand, so no nation could exist half slave and half free, he was simply acknowledging that the spoken words of the Son of God are unsurpassed and unsurpassable. When he suggested that the proposed inflated currency of the Union should have as the legend on each bill, "Silver and gold I have none, but what I have I give thee," (Acts 3, 6) he was not making sport of SS. Peter and John. He was drawing on the heritage of all Christians for the laudable purpose of making men smile.

Let me reiterate here what was said earlier, that Bible reading for the purpose of improving one's style or peppering one's speech with Scriptural references is the least worthy of all motivations. The process should be that, drawn by God's inspired word because it is his word, a man lets the Bible become a part of him. The centuries of preparation for Christ, the earthly life of the God-Man, the Mystical Christ, that is, the Church, in the first days of its spread, should be of the warp and woof of one's spiritual life. How can one expect to be remade in Christ—the task of all of us —except he first shall learn of him? And how great the risk of never coming close if a man continues to be satisfied with second and third-hand accounts of this man who made himself equal with God.

Christ is the key to the Old Testament Scriptures, the one in light of whom all the prophecies and hidden meanings, all the characters and events take on significance. "Never does the shadow exist before the body," writes Tertullian, "nor does the copy come before the original." Yet that is the central Christian fact, that Christ — the Messias who was to come—was prepared for in Jewish history, just as a masterpiece is preceded by a series of rough sketches. He is the "image of the Invisible God," (Col. 1, 15) the "first born of all creation," (Heb. 1, 3) the universal Exemplar. The whole old Law could say with the Baptist, "He who comes after me was made before me." "Late in historic time, but prior in priority to all time, Christ appears to us preceded by the shadows and the figures which

13

he himself had cast on Jewish history."[13] St. Augustine expressed the relation of the two parts of the Bible in this way: "The New Testament lies hidden in the Old: the Old becomes clear in the New." (*Q. in Heptat. lib.* 2, q. 73)

Jesus alone could "break the mysterious silence, provide the clue to the riddles of the prophets." He was the one keystone who could join the two arms of the arch of history as he was, too, the junction of the two peoples, Jewish and Gentile. The ecclesiastical writer Origen remarked long ago, "We who belong to the Catholic Church do not despise the Law of Moses, but accept it, so long as it is Jesus who interprets it for us. Only thus shall we understand it aright." (*In Jesu Nave, hom.* 9, n. 8) "In truth," he says elsewhere, "Scripture was the water: but since the coming of Jesus it has been turned for us into wine." (*In Exod.* h. 7, n. 1) And so when you pick up your Bible and begin to read, remember that the first part is shadowy symbol, figure, type; the second part is substance, reality, fulfillment. You read of Adam, Abraham, Moses, Jacob, David—look for Christ in each of them. Eve, Ruth, Esther, Judith, Anna the mother of Samuel—search for hints of Mary. The Garden of Paradise, the Ark, Mount Sinai: the Church is foreshadowed in them. The prophets—there you have the teaching Christ, suffering and doing for truth.

To conclude, let us imagine briefly that at the end of a business day marked by some measure of trial and temptation, you, an American lawyer and family man, discipline yourself to ten minutes of Bible reading. Somewhat skeptical of the spiritual aid to be found there, you open at random and read:

> See what airs they put on, the women folk of Sion, walk with heads held high, look about them with glancing eyes, click the trappings on their feet with mincing steps. Ay, but the Lord has his doom ready for them; bald of head and bare of temple the women of Sion shall know it. In one day the Lord shall sweep away all their finery, the shoes with the rest; locket and collar, necklace and bracelet and veil; hair-pin, ankle-ring, chain, scent-box, pendant, signet-ring and nose-ring; gala dress and gown and scarf, bodkin and mirror and shawl and riband and kerchief. There will be new fashions then; stench for scent, hempen

---

[13] Henri de Lubac, S.J., *Catholicism* (New York: Longmans, Green, 1950), p. 88. The citations that precede and follow this quotation are from the author's Chapter VI, "The Interpretation of Scripture," *passim*, pp. 83-106.

rope for waistband, baldness for curls, and hairshirt for
stomacher.   (Is. 3, 16-24)

With the modern appositeness of the words still ringing
in your ears, you turn to the New Testament and come on
this:

> I am rich, thou sayest. I have come into my own; noth-
> ing now is wanting to me. And all the while, if thou didst
> but know it, it is thou who art wretched, thou who art to
> be pitied. Thou art a beggar, and blind, and naked; and
> my counsel to thee is this, to come and buy from me what
> thou needest; gold . . . to make thee rich, and white
> garments, to clothe thee . . . rub salve, too, upon thy eyes,
> to restore them sight. It is those I love that I correct and
> chasten; kindle thy generosity and repent. See where I
> stand at the door, knocking; if anyone listens to my voice
> and opens the door, I will come in to visit him, and take
> my supper with him, and he shall sup with me. (Apoc. 3,
> 17-20)

The Lawyer and Christ

MSGR. WILLIAM H. RUSSELL, Ph. D.
Associate Professor of Religious Education
The Catholic University of America

The influence of the lawyer in shaping the destiny of America has been unique. It may be that his primary position is yielding in some degree to the business man or to the social scientist. But as long as our country remains a government of constitutional law the lawyer will be a leading citizen.

The lawyer is human. He is influenced by human frailty and the dominant notions of the day. The lawyer of 1776 accepted the natural law. The lawyer of 1951 is regarded in many legal circles as naive if he accepts that law. The philosophy of the individualistic state pervaded the mind of Justice Marshall. The philosophy of the collectivistic state may grip the lawyer of the future.

The lawyer is not the scientist, experimentating with this or that hypothesis. The lawyer is upholder of the law. However, he is confronted at present with the notion that law is the will of the majority, that law is what government or some bureau decrees, that law is what the dictator, known as man, decides is good for others. We all realize that there must be change and adaptation to changing conditions. Yet in the main the lawyer's task is that of discovering the permanent in the midst of change. He, much more than others, must have the strength to resist whim and passion and selfish, class-interest legislation, and secularism.

As Judge Dore eloquently observes[1] there is heard among the noisy strife of men an everlasting voice of immutability, the voice of reason and common sense. Law is an ordinance of reason. Human reason and the natural law are both based on divine reason, hence stability, permanence.

Because of that permanence we like to think of the lawyer, who has grasped the meaning of law, as a rocklike, steady, immovable character. We may ask, then, does the

---

[1] Edward S. Dore, "Human Rights and the Law", *Fordham Law Review*, XV (March, 1946), 3-18.

study of law generate within itself the power to impart rocklike strength to the lawyer? Undoubtedly, the secret of strength within men varies from man to man. He who develops a proper love of justice will indeed shine as a beacon light within his community. Aside from that, may I cite one historical incident in relation to this matter of moral strength required to reach into and expose the deceits, the prejudices of the modern world? Jefferson rises monumentally among American lawyers. He was of course the center of controversy in his day. Many so-called religious people bitterly opposed him. I make no defense here of his Deism, of his mistaken belief in the power of human reason alone to guide men's lives. I refer to the historical fact that Jefferson the lawyer went outside the law to build his own sturdiness of character. It came from the men he admired in his youth, and from his composition of what is known, rather arrogantly of course, as the Jefferson Bible. He culled from the Gospels what he thought was best in the sayings of Christ.

That incident suggests the fittingness of our theme—Christ and the lawyer. What a field for life-long investigation on the part of the individual lawyer! In this essay I have in mind not the literary influence of the Bible, nor even the general subject of religion. The discussion of law as such comes only indirectly within our specific aim. I am limiting our all-too-cursory examination to the question of contact of character upon character, of the entire Person of Christ and his outlook on the lawyer who persists in gazing upon the Nazarene. Christ in his human nature is the most inspiring picture of manhood ever offered to the lawyer as man, as Christian, as member of the mystical body, as friend of Christ. It is my conviction, for instance, that only in proportion as the lawyer looks beyond the Law, as he participates in Christ's thinking will he fully grasp the significance of the principles set forth in the second paragraph of the Declaration of Independence. I realize that it has become intellectually fashionable to reject the truths enunciated as self-evident in that document. Fortunately truth has a way of surviving, especially when it is viewed in him who is Truth eternal. Again, the lawyer who wishes to develop in his own character that rare balance of justice and mercy can find nowhere the balance demonstrated by Jesus.

17

One problem for the lawyer is that of acquiring the legal mind without becoming a legalist. It is always possible for the just judge, as well as for the man of principle, to become hard and unbending. There are those who would put human nature in a strait-jacket. There come to our minds the American Puritan and what were called the Blue Laws for the Sabbath. I make reference to the type of character that originated the Blue Laws merely as an illustration of the type of mind that confronted Christ, namely, the pharisaical mind. The Pharisee in the century before Christ was strict but just. By the time of Christ he had begun to boast of his righteousness, and he sought to strait-jacket human nature through his minute Sabbath regulations. He had degenerated into the legalist.

The Gospel reader early becomes aware of the frequency with which Jesus cured people on the Sabbath. The law forbade any work on that day. I choose by way of example the occasion, in Jerusalem, when Christ walked up to a crippled beggar who for 38 years had been waiting for a cure. Jesus said to him: "Rise, take up thy pallet (a bed of straw) and walk." Immediately the cured man began to walk. (Jn. 5, 8) The Pharisees met him, and accused him thus: "It is the Sabbath; thou art not allowed to take up thy pallet." The miraculous cure made no impression on them! Their own laws were being flaunted. Later, when they learned that it was Jesus who had done the curing, the narrative informs us: "This is why the Jews kept persecuting Jesus, because he was doing these things on the Sabbath." They accused him of breaking the law, because to them the letter was more important than the spirit. On another occasion, when Jesus gave sight to the blind man, the charge made against him was this: "This man is not from God, for he does not keep the Sabbath." (Jn. 9, 16)

The miracles of Jesus were good deeds, done for the benefit of suffering humanity. The Mosaic Law had never intended that good should not be done on the Sabbath. Law is an ordinance of reason. But the Pharisees were not interested in the spirit of the Mosaic Law. Their whole concern was casuistry or their own petty interpretations. Conflict between that type of mind and the mind of Jesus was inevitable. The lawyer who studies these acts of Christ will never become the legalist. "The Sabbath was made for man, and not man for the Sabbath." (Mk. 2, 27)

Hypocrisy may enter into the lives of any of us. However, the legalist, the self-righteous individual who wants society to develop along the lines of his own petty schemes seems most readily to degenerate from the state of being a little god into that of being a first-class hypocrite. The twenty-third chapter of St. Matthew is filled with Christ's "woes" uttered against the Pharisees and lawyers. Courage was required to expose those in the seats of power. "Woe to you scribes and Pharisees . . . (You) have left undone the weightier matter of the Law, right judgment and mercy and faith. . . . Blind guides, who strain out the gnat but swallow the camel. . . . You clean the outside of the cup and the dish, but within they are full of robbery and uncleanness. . . . You are like whited sepulchres, which outwardly appear to men beautiful . . . and you also outwardly appear just to men, but within are full of hypocrisy and iniquity." Those are, to be sure, strong words, words that arouse hatred. Does not each lawyer, however, know of graft within his own community, and graft that goes unexposed because of a fear of the grafters? Not all of the fearlessness of the Nazarene can take root in us, but more association with him would engender some power of indignation against public corruption. And lest it be thought that the Jesus who uttered those woes was too harsh, let it be remembered that it was this same Jesus who was merciful to the woman of sin brought to him by the same Pharisees. He combined love of justice with the quality of mercy.

Love of justice; courage to stand up for justice! How difficult it is! Let your imagination roam backward to all the instances of mob violence or of public hysteria annihilating justice in this country. Notable examples of fearless, courageous judges standing for human rights there have been. But negroes know how justice runs for cover when mobs take over. The hysteria aroused over Lincoln's death resulted in some who were really innocent being put to death. At present, in the necessary search for communists who have infiltrated into the government, it is possible that some innocent people have been accused. Therefore the problem that the lawyer has to ponder is what he would do in the face of a mob, or when his friends desert him one by one because of public pressure.

Should not every lawyer read the life of St. Thomas More? Better than that, should not every lawyer study the actions of Christ? Christ never waited, as does the politician, to see which way the wind is blowing. Look into the sixth chapter of St. John and observe how Jesus, in the face of opposition, calmly continued with his teaching. He was tremendously popular when he fed the multitudes with the loaves and fishes. On the next day, however, when he proposed the doctrine of the Holy Eucharist these erstwhile enthusiasts for him said: "This is a hard saying. Who can listen to it?" And the account informs us that, "From this time many of his disciples turned back and no longer went about with him." Did Jesus retreat? Did he soften his statements? No, indeed, He even turned to his best friends, and put this decision up to them: "Do you also wish to go away?" There he is—the unfaltering Man, the Man of courage and conviction, the challenging Man, the Man who strengthens those who come to him. In fact, no more courageous face has ever been painted than this description of Jesus by Luke the physician as Jesus prepared to go up to Jerusalem to his martyrdom: "He steadfastly set his face to go to Jerusalem." (9, 51)

Courage is required to defend the weak against the strong. Jesus had such courage. Only the courageous man can expose the tyrannically strong. Jesus did it. But how about holding up under that tension year after year? What will happen when those who are professedly religious join forces with the unscrupulous, the haters of religion against one who tries to live by the truth? Did Jesus live under this tension? Early in his career we find this notation: "The Pharisees went out and took counsel with the Herodians against him, how they might do away with him." (Mk. 3, 6) Do away with him! What an atmosphere in which to live! The Pharisees were supposed to stand for God, for strict religion. The Herodians were lax, ecclesiastical politicians, followers of Herod. The mutual hatred between Pharisee and Herodian was fused into a common hatred against the Galilean.

Is there not something parallel in our own country at the present time? The communists are the sworn enemies of

20

God and the United States. They assert that religion is linked with capitalism. What is puzzling is that some in this country who call themselves Christian, who profess to believe in God, are apparently willing to line up with the communists against the Church. We have had the strange sight of a communist editor of a religious paper. No doubt many of these people are duped by the communists. All of us are in duty bound to fight against the injustices of capitalism. Granted that, one doubts that it is love of communism that induces some American religious leaders to shout that Rome is the enemy. The keen lawyer will discover also that there was a reason for excluding the name of God at the founding of the U. N. Is that law which excludes parochial school children from riding on public school buses in many of our States an ordinance of reason? Or is there some other motive behind the law? It seems that God, like the Declaration of Independence, is out of date! The American people as a whole believe in God. But what the McCollum case amounts to is that an atheist boy should not be embarrassed, and hence other children have to be deprived of their right to hear about God. More than once in history the leaders of the people have betrayed the people. And no betrayal is ever so dangerous to any nation as that which seeks to transfer authority from God to human dictators.

I wish to go on record as believing that Christ has many fine, earnest and sincere followers among all sects. I am not concerned, however, directly with those followers. Rather I am thinking of the aid the lawyer could offer to such followers. He, by his training, is better prepared to examine into the effort in the U. S. at present to keep God out of the lives of the people. This effort may be detected as the motivation of many who invoke, hypocritically, the letter of the law and the assistance of the judicial process. The lawyer has to scrutinize the hidden reasons among those who seek to block released time for religion in the schools. The bulk, the majority of the American people are sound. Among the molders of public opinion, however, one detects that through the classroom, through the publishing houses, through the newspapers there filters that propaganda against Christ, against God. Many seek to cover up their malice through a smear campaign againt the

Church, alleging that the hierarchy has political ambitions. Let us look at a comparison. If you wish to understand the aim of Russia, study the accusations it makes. It accuses us of imperialism. Imperialism is precisely its own goal. Likewise the followers of Christ here are accused of political chicanery. It is the accusers who bear watching. More than one American secularist would rejoice at the arrival of the day when it would be a crime to mention the name of God.

Often in history the arrogance and even the hypocrisy of Christians have turned well-intentioned people away from Christianity. Let us grant all of that. The lawyer of experience will learn that it does not explain the effort in America to blot out Christ from the hearts of the young. Present propaganda may be understood by analyzing the type of social pressure used against the Nazarene. On the one hand, anyone who professed that he was truly the Messias, the Christ, was to be put out of the synagogue. (Jn. 9, 22) On the other hand this type of argument was employed: "Has any of the rulers believed in him, or any of the Pharisees? But this crowd, which does not know the Law, is accursed." (Jn. 7, 48) That refrain would be changed today to this: Does any scientist believe in him? Certainly, many scientists believe in him. The lawyer simply has to realize that the type of argument continues. He may be sneered at, or even shouted down, if he should stand up for Christ. In fact, one of the very Pharisees stood up and said: "Does our law judge any man unless it first give him a hearing, and know what he does?" Back came the sneer: "Art thou also a Galilean", which means, a rustic, a nit-wit, or a stupid lawyer!

Verily the lawyer of today who takes Christ as his ideal will arouse the ire of those who desire the triumph of communism. Return with me again to Jerusalem. The Jews were a theocratic people in that they were under the direct government of God. He alone was to be the object of their worship. What we call civil government was in their practice under the religious. But pagan Rome had conquered Palestine. In Roman politics likewise there was no separation of Church and State. In Rome the emperor was supreme. The secular ruled the religious. Being strict Jews, the Pharisees taught that it was wrong to pay tribute to Rome. Roman money could not be used in the temple services. Rome was very jealous, very touchy on this matter of taxes. Conveniently for the moment, the Pharisees forgot their hatred of Rome, and although they had time and again failed to entrap Jesus, they played their trump card toward the end of his life. Knowing that Pilate, the Roman governor, would have his spies among the crowds in Jerusalem, the Pharisees sent their agents to trick Jesus through the political question. They began with this flattery: "Master, we know that thou teachest and speakest rightly, and showest no favor to anyone, but teachest the way of God in truth." (That flattery at least tells us what the common opinion of Jesus was.) Then they sprang this trap, in the presence of a large crowd: "Is it lawful for us to give tribute to Caesar, or not?"

The lonely Galilean became the cynosure of all eyes. After exposing their hypocrisy, he said: "Show me a denarius", which was a Roman coin. In carrying it they objectively admitted they were paying tribute to Rome. He simply asked: "Whose image and inscription is this?" Answering they said: "Caesar's." He replied: "Render, therefore, to Caesar the things that are Caesar's, and to God the things that are God's." (Mt. 22, 21) Marvelling at the depth, the simplicity of the reply, the enemies of Jesus paid him the apt tribute of silence. He had expressed a truth which was to revolutionize Church-State relations. Henceforth it would be, not either or, but true allegiance to both. The State has its rights; citizens owe allegiance to the State. God also has his rights. Will the lawyer become an American secularist if he ponder that statement of the Son of God? Will he sell out the U. S. to Russia? Even though he sees that social change is necessary, will he substitute himself or the State for God?

I repeat, the lawyer, layman that he be, may be in our own day confronted by the sight of so-called churchmen, with an itch for publicity, who would sell out their God. Just a few weeks after Christ had originated that famous statement he was turned over to the Roman procurator with this accusation: "We have found this man perverting the nation, and forbidding the payment of taxes to Caesar, and saying that he is Christ the king." (Lu. 23, 2) Yes, those people of a theocracy, in their hatred of Jesus, rejected their God with this remark: "We have no king but Caesar."

(Jn. 19, 15) In the blindness brought on by their hatred of Christ's Church, some churchmen would say with the communists: We have no king but the State.

Indeed history repeats itself. What Christ met, the lawyer of today will meet. The lawyer is accustomed to meet perjury in the courts. He is puzzled, however, by the finesse with which perjury has come to be practiced. Hitler and the communists have perfected the technique. We live in the age of the exaltation of the lie. The lawyer as well as the average citizen is often baffled in his efforts to uncover the lie. As a psychological study the Hiss case will go down in history.

Likewise it is interesting to hear, from some of those strongly suspected of disloyalty to their country, that it would be impossible for them to be traitors because they are descended from ancient American families. Page through the Gospels. One finds there men who boasted of their ancestry, of their descent from Abraham: "We are the children of Abraham, and we have never been slaves to anyone." (Jn. 8, 33) These are the men who were scandalized at the actions of Jesus. "Why does your Master eat with publicans and sinners?" (Mt. 9, 11) Little did those proud descendants of Abraham realize what had been taking place in their own character. It was a shock to them to hear this truth from one who knows the hidden influences shaping the thoughts of men: "The father from whom you are is the devil, and the desires of your father it is your will to do. He was a murderer from the beginning, and has not stood in the truth because there is no truth in him. When he tells a lie he speaks from his very nature, for he is a liar and the father of lies." (Jn. 8, 44) We all know that it is unfashionable at present to believe in the devil, but for that very reason it is all the more important that the lawyer examine the evidence put forward by Jesus of Nazareth that there is a devil. Is it not significant that an age that boasts that it has eliminated the devil is at the same time the age that exalts the lie?[2]

And how may the lawyer avoid that greatest of all deceptions that there is no devil? In his own manner of living Christ the Man is a pattern for all of us. His basic rule is:

---

[2] "The devil will never be raised from the dead." N. Schmidt, *The Prophet of Nazareth*, New York: Macmillan, 1905, p. 346.

24

Keep God first and foremost in your life. Loyalty to God will protect the lawyer from worship of the lie. The habits, the ambitions of men drive them in directions of which they are not always fully conscious. Any lawyer will profit from an analysis of the threefold effort of the devil to entrap Christ at the beginning of his career. The first temptation was this: Put food or sensualism ahead of obedience to God. The second was: Presume that since you are clever you can bribe the judge or policeman, or that friends in high places will protect you. It is the third temptation that is most revealing. In effect the devil promised Christ Wall St., the R. F. C., Hollywood, London, Paris, Moscow, and the atom bomb—all on one condition: "If thou wilt fall down and worship me." (Mt. 4, 9) Wise the lawyer, or any individual, who has plumbed the significance of that temptation. Safe is the leader of men who will prayerfully ponder Christ's fiery, indignant, scorching answer: "Begone, Satan. The Lord thy God shalt thou worship and him only shalt thou serve." Yes, Christ knows what the desire for power will do to a man's character. No follower of Christ will ever worship the father of lies. Only the Christlike lawyer will acquire the acumen to expose the false gods of a nation.

Lawyers of course often disagree. That is to be expected. It is not always easy to discern just where justice may be found in a particular case. Respect always goes out to that lawyer who honestly believes in the justice of his case and sturdily argues against his opponent. On the other hand our notions of justice may be colored by social, educational, economic or political background. Unbeknown to ourselves we may have a distorted view of justice. Here the Nazarene can be of assistance. "You shall know the truth, and the truth shall make you free." (Jn. 8, 32) The friend of Christ does not of course obtain omniscience. He is not shielded from mistakes nor even from sin. But Christ does put conscience into the lawyer. It was conscience that finally saved Whittaker Chambers. Many a lobbyist in Washington would have twinges of conscience if he placed himself daily at the feet of the divine teacher. Christ keeps his true friends free from class views, from narrowness, from that distortion known as secularism.

To be a man of integrity the lawyer must face certain hazards. The poor, the widowed, the unhappy will flock to

25

his office, and as a consequence he faces the hazard of poverty. Around him will be many who trim their principles and advance financially. Certain predatory interests, even gangsters, if they find him opposing them, may threaten him and malign him. Human applause may seldom be his. Flaming headlines may not fill up his scrapbook. In the midst of the calumnies heaped upon him, there may arise from the crowd, as there did for the Nazarene, that voice of a woman's intuition: "Blessed is the womb that bore thee." (Lu. 11, 27) Happy mother who has you for a Son! To acquire that moral majesty that over-rides selfish opposition, the lawyer has only to recall the impression made by Jesus on the police sent on one occasion to arrest him: "Never has man spoken as this man." (Jn. 7, 46)

Indeed there are compensations for the lawyer who decides that side by side with his study of the Law there will go that more thrilling study of the character of Jesus. The lawyer will experience what Peter experienced, namely, that Christ opens up, as it were, to loyal friends, and the lawyer will say with Peter: "Lord, it is good for us to be here." (Mt. 17, 4) No leader so touches the chords of loyalty as does this Man who is a contemporary of every man. Let us examine the case of the hard-headed Thomas. His disbelief after the resurrection has earned for him, somewhat unfairly, the title of the doubting Thomas. If one looks into the eleventh chapter of St. John one will discover another side of this Thomas. Christ had withdrawn twenty miles from Jerusalem because of hatred toward him and because his "hour" had not yet come. Forgetful of the danger to him in Jerusalem, the two sisters of the dying Lazarus sent this message to Jesus: "Lord, he whom thou lovest is sick." (How like a woman to express it in that manner!) Would Christ brave danger for a friend? Would Christ prove loyal? When he proposed to the apostles to return to Jerusalem they attempted to dissuade him, reminding him that just previously in Jerusalem they "were seeking to stone thee; and dost thou go there again?" Unflinchingly, firmly came this decision: "Let us go to him." Loyalty arouses loyalty. When hard-headed Thomas observed the loyalty of Jesus to Lazarus, Thomas said to the others: "Let us also go, that we may die with him." Yes, to

26

be associated with Jesus of Nazareth does something to the lawyer.

Startling, divine claims were made by this carpenter from Nazareth. He invites the lawyer to examine those claims. No arrogance will be found there. Surrounded indeed he was from the first with hatred and malice. Never did hate take root in his heart. "Father, forgive them." Fearless, self-reliant was Jesus. Jesus likewise was docile and a Man of prayer. No man could intimidate him. Little children ran into his arms. The ruler who signed his death-warrant declared: "I am innocent of the blood of this just man."

The poise, balance, symmetry of that very human character could not have been invented by the highest artistry of a Shakespeare. Only once in history did God become Man. He was born "to bear witness to the truth." (Jn. 18, 37) And it is the truth that he is available to the lawyer today. In the lonely and often discouraging battle for the truth, for justice one may ask what is the advantage of having Christ. One answer is this: "He who eats my flesh . . . abides in me and I in him." (Jn. 6, 57) What a privilege to have the same Jesus who looked through the soul of Peter and won him. "Abide in me, and I in you." (Jn. 15, 4) The Catholic lonely! Never. "I have called you friends, because all things that I have heard from my Father I have made known to you." (Jn. 15, 15) The American man or woman who wishes to learn how to win a friend and keep him has only to put himself or herself in the company of him who said: "These things I have spoken to you that my joy may be in you, and that your joy may be made full." (Jn. 15, 11)

Democracy and Responsibility

FENTON MORAN
Executive Secretary: William J. Kerby Foundation

The world in which we live today is dominated by a problem in semantics: What is the meaning of the word democracy? Now, perhaps I ought to begin over again by trying to answer another question: What is the meaning of the word semantics? Semantics, as far as I am able to gather, is a rather mysterious science dealing basically with the meaning of words. But because words like the human beings who use them are constantly undergoing change, shifting their relationships to one another and to other things, mere dictionary meanings do not suffice to cover the complex field of the relationship between people and words, which is the proper field of semantics. Thus, for example, the dictionary gives as the definition of the word in which we are interested, democracy, "government by the people," deriving this meaning from the sense of the two Greek words which make it up, *demos,* the people, and *kratein,* to rule. We quickly perceive the inadequacy of this simple understanding of the word. An indication of how far the word democracy has strayed from the straight and narrow path of literal meaning is provided by the invention in eastern Europe of the expression "a people's democracy." It is as though they felt in that part of the world that the concept conveyed by the word democracy alone had become anaemic and they have given it a sort of blood transfusion in the form of the reinforcing word people's.

With words behaving in this wayward fashion, we summon to our assistance the science of semantics. Semantics is concerned with what I should call the two-way relationship between people and words, the influence which people have on the meaning of words and the influence which words have on the lives of people. Throughout the world men are seeking to draw out the meaning of this word democracy, or to impose their own special understandings on the word. And in its turn the word never leaves off exerting a tremendous influence on the lives of men. I think that we can say, therefore, that this word democracy

28

is an eminently semantic word, although by this time I may be giving you the impression that this is an eminently pedantic discussion. I regret that aspect of it, but I do not see, really, quite how it could be avoided. If we wish to have a firm grasp of the ideas which are important in our lives, we must first take hold of the words which express these ideas and which have an influence on the ideas themselves. If we do not master the words, the words will very quickly tend to master us, and there is no tyranny in the world comparable to the despotism of words when these become instruments in the hands of skillful manipulators.

In his telling satire, *Animal Farm,* George Orwell gives us a demonstration of the modern technique of word-manipulation. This present-day fable relates how a community of domestic animals, under the leadership of the pigs (apparently regarded by Orwell as the cleverest of the farm animals), revolt against their human masters, drive them out and take over the management of the farm themselves. Gradually the managerial function is absorbed more and more completely by the clever pigs, until finally the other animals find themselves working for the pigs exactly as they had previously worked for the human owners of the farm. The revolution begins by laying down the great basic principle that "All animals are equal." In the end, when the pigs have taken over completely, we see that this great revolutionary device has been amended by imperceptible stages to read: "All animals are equal, but some animals are more equal than others."

At a time when there is so much confusion in the world over the meaning of this word democracy, when whole sections of the human race are prepared to fly at one another's throats over this word, I think that it is urgent for us Americans to remind ourselves that we do not really have to look beyond the end of our own noses for the answer to the question with which we began this discussion. Because the best, and the most complete, and the most workable definition of democracy is to be found in a home-grown document to which our country has been endeavoring for some hundred and seventy-five years to give practical social expression. I am referring to the Declaration of Independence. I would ask you to consider this document which was signed for all of us in 1776.

The essence of the Declaration, or in any case the only part of its content which interests us here, is contained in the first paragraph and the first half of the second paragraph. The balance of the document, the long recital of grievances against the British Crown by which the Colonists justified their separation from Britain, is not relevant today and has only an historical interest. The two paragraphs to which I invite your attention, on the other hand, contain the permanent philosophical concepts without which, I submit, our democracy could not exist. Let us examine these paragraphs each in turn.

> When in the course of human events, it becomes necessary for one people to dissolve the political bands which have connected them with another, and to assume among the Powers of the earth, the separate and equal station to which the Laws of Nature and of Nature's God entitle them, a decent respect to the opinions of mankind requires that they should declare the causes which impel them to the separation.

There are, it seems to me, two important ideas contained in this paragraph. First, the separate and equal station which is claimed for the states represented by the signers of the Declaration is made to depend on the Laws of Nature and of Nature's God. The authors of the Declaration were not speaking on their own authority in this document. They were not asserting the right to independence on any material ground. They were not saying, as it is the fashion to say nowadays of colonial peoples, that they had grown up and were ready for self-government. They were not claiming independence because they felt that they had the force to sustain this claim. They were merely bowing before a necessity imposed upon them by the Laws of Nature and of Nature's God. For them, in view of the human events which preceded their action, it would be a failure in duty to the higher law not to assume the responsibilities of nationhood. It seems to me that we have here a plain acknowledgement of the total dependency of human affairs on the designs of the Creator. Thus we see that the very point of departure of this basic charter of our democracy is not primarily an assertion of human rights; it is an acknowledgement of human duty towards the Lawgiver who has the government of all human events. The lawyer must learn from this Lawmaker.

30

The second important point which I see in this paragraph is found in the motive given for formulating the Declaration: "a decent respect to the opinions of mankind." It seems to me that in this the authors of the Declaration were inspired by a vision outstripping their own time by centuries. They were acting as citizens of the world, as members of a human community of which the essential solidarity was very largely obscured for their contemporaries by the narrowest sort of national interests. The Declaration of Independence was not addressed primarily to the American people in whose name it was promulgated, nor even to the British Crown or the British people, the other party most directly concerned in the event which it proclaimed. The Declaration was directed to a "candid world" in order that the whole of mankind might know the causes of the action taken and judge of the rightness of that action. The independence of the Colonies could ultimately have been achieved without any apologia such as the Declaration. The blood and sacrifices of the Colonists which won their freedom from the onerous dominion of George III would have sufficed for the actual liberation of the states. But because they felt that their struggle had likewise to be won on a moral plane, that the material victory of which, in that dark hour, they could not even have been over-confident, would not be enough to complete their purpose, the authors of the Declaration felt required to state their cause for the opinion of all men. It would seem to me that we have in this an indication of faith in the universal character of democracy and a kind of foreshadowing of the world-wide organization of mankind towards which I believe that we must hope that the United Nations represents at least a permanent, irreversible step.

The first paragraph of the Declaration with these two major points which I have stressed constitutes a sort of paving of the way, an introduction to the great dominant idea which is to follow. With the second paragraph we are plunged into the very heart of the matter. The sentences which compose the first half of this paragraph contain the whole of the law and the prophets of our democracy. They say in prose which is lean as it is vigorous all that need be said about the philosophical structure of democracy.

31

> We hold these truths to be self-evident, that all men are created equal, that they are endowed by their Creator with certain unalienable Rights, that among these are Life, Liberty, and the pursuit of Happiness. That to secure these rights, Governments are instituted among Men, deriving their just powers from the consent of the governed.

These words set the real tone of our democracy which is a high faith in human destiny. There the lawyer is invited to look beyond the Law. It must come as a shock to some people to realize, as they are obliged to realize in reading this language, that this essential core of the Declaration is sheer dogma. It does not reason with us about the statements which it makes. It advances no arguments in support of the principles upon which it builds. It describes these quite flatly as "self-evident truths". If you are not agreed that they are self-evident, or if you feel that they stand in need of some demonstration, the authors of the Declaration will not take the time to debate the matter with you. If you wish to follow the reasoning of the Declaration through to its full conclusion—in other words, if you want to give reality to the human ideal of democracy, here, according to the Declaration, are the basic, irreducible assumptions you must be prepared to make: 1. Equal creation of all men. 2. Inalienable rights conferred upon all men by their Creator. 3. The chief function of governments to subserve the rights of men.

These three assumptions being so important for the structure of democracy, let us look at them more closely and try to satisfy ourselves about what they mean. To attempt to build a democratic society while ignoring them or failing to understand their significance would be like building a vast cathedral while taking no account of the laws of physics governing stresses and strains.

"That all men are created equal." What on earth could this mean? By any standards which we are in a position to apply to human beings, the inequality of men, the diversity of their endowments, is one of the most striking features we can perceive. Materially, socially, physically, mentally, morally, men come into the world and move through it under tremendous handicaps, or with tremendous advantages in regard to their fellow men. What did the authors of the Declaration mean, then, when they proclaimed the equality of all men to be a self-evident truth? Since men

32

are so glaringly unequal in all the fields which we can observe, we are obliged to conclude either that Thomas Jefferson and his colleagues were fools or dupes or liars, or that in their Declaration they were considering men on a plane on which human equality is a reality. I am certain that the immense majority of our fellow Americans would angrily reject the first of these conclusions; the men who brought our nation into existence could not have been fools or dupes or liars. But where, then, is the plane on which their assertion of human equality is true?

I submit that the only rational answer to this question is that this plane is the plane of the Creator Himself. In their proclamation of human equality, the authors of the Declaration were endeavouring to see men as their Maker sees them. In the face of the overwhelming act of power of the Creator in bringing human persons into existence, the minor differences among men on the temporal planes to which I have referred fade into insignificance. In the eyes of God, who bestows or withholds qualities, talents, gifts, fortune, honors—the accidents of human personality—in accordance with his own impenetrable designs, all men *are* equal as his creatures and his children. We see, then, that the very first assumption required by the Declaration for belief in democracy is concerned not at all with a political question, or even a social question. It is concerned with a question belonging properly in the domain of theology, the relationship existing among men as a result of their relationship to their Maker.

"That they are endowed by their Creator with certain unalienable Rights." The modern controversy over the meaning of democracy is accompanied by a contingent debate on the nature and origin of human rights. What rights belong to man, and from whence do they come?

The Declaration limits its answer to the first of these questions to a rather general description of these rights as "certain" and "unalienable". But there is no possibility of mistaking the categorical answer which it gives to the second question. The rights of man originate with God. They are of a piece with the same mysterious design which brings the Creator to make all men equal. They are, as it were, the measure of that equality. The equality of men recognized by the Declaration is not a reduction of all mankind to the lowest common denominator, a leveling off of human beings to the status of anonymous digits without significance and without personality. By the fact of an endowment of inalienable rights this equality on the contrary lifts all men up to the highest degree of the creation which we know. Without regard to individual worth which we are able to measure in terms of perceptible traits, every man has an intrinsic value which lies beyond these traits. It is his dignity which makes him worthy of the Creator's act in bestowing these imprescriptible rights upon him.

The third basic assumption required by the Declaration for belief in democracy is subsidiary to the first two we have just been considering. It is a kind of practical implementation of these two. "That to secure these rights, Governments are instituted among men, deriving their just powers from the consent of the governed." If you accept the first two assumptions: human equality and inalienable human rights, I do not see any reasonable ground upon which to quarrel with the third. In the first two propositions the Declaration unmistakably affirms the primacy of human personality, the essential central importance of the individual human person in the scheme governing the conduct of human affairs. All organization tending to implement this scheme must, therefore, subserve the human person. The literal language of the Declaration limiting the reason for being of governments to the securing of human rights would tend too greatly to narrow the field of legitimate functions of government. Governments have likewise in the natural order the functions of restraining men to the necessities of order and justice, of making the exercise of their rights compatible with the well-being of their fellow men, of giving reality to the Christian ideal of the brotherhood of men, of helping men to be good. But all of these functions, very far from obscuring, tend rather to emphasize that the end of society is man, and not the end of man society; that the State exists for men and their service, and not men primarily for the service of the State.

In this necessarily sketchy analysis of the Declaration I have been endeavoring to extract its essence. I hope that I may have succeeded in some measure in bringing out into relief the few basic principles which it emphasizes and which were intended as the foundation upon which our

34

democracy should rest. Certainly, the chief purpose of the Declaration was to make these principles clear to the world. But it would be a mistake to believe that the whole function of the Declaration ended with this. The men who composed and signed this great document were not merely philosophers speculating in an ivory tower on the meaning of human destiny. They were practical men, men of action, men of great courage. They did not content themselves with setting down on paper the ideal principles which ought to govern a just society. Their Declaration is more than a profession of belief; it is likewise a program of action designed to give reality to this belief.

Let us skip down through the text of the Declaration, not pausing to take in the list of sins of commission and omission of the King of England. We jump in this manner over the concluding portion of the second paragraph and twenty-nine subsequent paragraphs describing the specific grievances of the Colonies. We come then to paragraph number 32, the last one in the document. This paragraph solemnly proclaims the dissolution of all political ties between Great Britain and the Colonies and the right of those Colonies henceforth to do all acts pertaining to free and sovereign states. It then concludes with this deeply moving and immensely practical sentence, immediately preceding the signatures of the members of the Continental Congress:

> And for the support of this Declaration, with a firm reliance on the Protection of Divine Providence, we mutually pledge to each other our Lives, or Fortunes, and our sacred Honour.

Fifty-six men—many of whom we can remember today only as their odd archaic names appearing on this faded parchment—fifty-six men were prepared to sacrifice their dearest possessions for the support of what they believed to be right. They felt so strongly about the principles they had enunciated that they would prefer not to enjoy their fortunes and their honour, indeed not even to go on living in a world in which these principles could not prevail. In this conclusion then we find the practical test of the validity of the convictions professed in the opening part of the Declaration. The authors of this document were not content with believing and proclaiming their belief. They

35

wished to activate this belief and on the success of this action they staked everything that men hold most dear.

How do you think that we measure up today to this high purpose? Do we still believe what the authors of the Declaration believed, and if so are we too prepared to support this belief by pledging to one another our lives, our fortunes and our sacred honour?

The men who gave us the Declaration as a rallying point for our political faith to this day challenged in their proclamation of freedom the greatest political and military power of their time, Britain, omnipotent on the seas and unbeaten on land in the wars of that century. The men who put their signatures at the bottom of the Declaration of Independence took on a truly formidable enemy when they provoked war with the British Crown. But if we wish to live up to their high example and to defend the principles to which they pledged their lives, fortunes and honour, we must be prepared to pledge our own for the support of these same principles against an enemy infinitely more powerful and incomparably more resourceful than that poor stick George III. The enemy we face is not a single great military and political power like the majesty of Britain at the close of the XVIIIth century. He does not place in the open field against us soldiers whose scarlet coats would make it easy for us to identify them. He has not, as a matter of fact, so far really engaged us in a full military contest. But the undeclared war with him exists just as really as the shots that were fired on Bunker Hill.

Who is this enemy?

At the close of the first World War there appeared in an effective role on the world stage a new personage of the drama who challenged every hitherto accepted political and social belief of men throughout the world. In his penetrating study of the dilemma of the modern world, *The Revolt of the Masses,* the Spanish philosopher, José Ortega y Gasset, identified this personage and gave him a name. Ortega calls him *hombre masa,* literally mass man. He is the collectivity considered as a personality. He is the enemy. He would transfer to himself from you and me all the objectives and solicitudes of society. He would make the collectivity the beneficiary of all the fruits of the social processes which, in our democratic view, ought to be directed towards the human person. His declaration would be a paraphrase of the words of 1776 somewhat as follows: "We hold these historical surmises to be experimentally demonstrable. That all men are engendered in equal insignificance. That they are endowed by the collectivity with short-term, revocable privileges. That among these are life, for so long as it may be profitable to the State, liberty to act and to think as the State decrees, and the pursuit of the aggrandizement of the collectivity."

Unlike our own founding fathers, *hombre masa* did not come out openly and plainly with this program of belief. He is too subtle and too versed in the ways of the world for such frankness. He sought the allegiance of men worn out by the excesses of modern history through a beguiling gospel of complete repose for the weary individual in the security of the collectivity. In the place of that ancient "opium of the people" as he calls it, reliance on Divine Providence, he proposed a modern narcotic, reliance on the total providence of the State. Away with the nightmare of a life burdened with individual decisions and individual responsibilities! away with the facsimile of liberty chaining man within the narrow confines of conscience and charity! away with that exhausting and most frustrating of deceptions, the pursuit of happiness! Come unto me all ye who are burdened with the insupportable cares of individual existence and I will give you rest in the obliteration of the collectivity.

Is it any wonder that millions of bewildered humans were quickly lured by this promise of escape from the chains and scourges of the condition in which we human beings exist? In Russia the new gospel was imposed with a baptism of fire and blood. In Germany and elsewhere it penetrated deeply into the consciousness of weary, disillusioned people. It spread, and it continues to spread in a human soil richly prepared for it by the loss of faith in ancient values, seen by men as masks for hypocrisy, by the blindness and ineptness of selfish leaders, by the detachment of democratic societies from the principles which give them life. The progress of *hombre masa* is the tragic measure of the bankruptcy and failure of the democratic ideal.

This new doctrine of repose in the collectivity pretends to be an invitation to a permanent escape from the anguish and servitudes of the human condition. How alluring it is for men tormented by the unending need to choose, to decide, to assume responsibility! Here is a life of peace in which choices are made, decisions taken, responsibilities all assumed by the collectivity. Just let yourself live. To live, from a positive verb of action, the act of being, becomes a verb of the passive voice without any object beyond its visible limits. Ultimately the doctrine of *hombre masa* is the doctrine of Nirvana, the loss of the human person in the dreamless sleep of the collectivity.

It is, I should think, precisely on this ground of escape from the need for being, completely and individually, that the doctrine of *hombre masa* marks its furthest departure from the ideal of democracy. Because democracy, with its insistence on the central importance of the human person, involves the most heroic facing by the individual of all the issues of existence. Democracy is all the contrary of an escapism. Democracy thrusts on the individual human person all his share of the burden of the condition in which human beings exist. Democracy faces the ultimate fact that human life is not a dream, that human life is a test, a trial, a struggle. Democracy exalts the human person, recognizing in every man unquestionable titles to equality and inalienable rights. Democracy gives stature and grandeur to all of us. But it does this in order to prepare us to confront reality, to contend with the life we must lead which is, as every article of our Christian faith tells us, an agony— an agony in the strict etymological sense of a trial of strength, a contest for a prize to be won.

So in the last analysis it is not because *hombre masa* tells us that we can no longer own property or clip coupons or indulge the changing whims of our nature that we must reject his overtures with violence. It it because he would take from us our final and most precious right, that which makes us human persons, that which gives us ground for action in common with our Brother and Lord and Saviour, Jesus Christ—the right to suffer. Democracy like Christianity is made of stern stuff. Democracy demands that we have the courage and the grandeur to live.

Does all this sound like fanatical austerity? I put it to you that it is only a realistic recognition of the parallel— I should almost be tempted to say the identity between the ideals of democracy and those of Christianity. The world of Joseph Stalin and of Mao Tse-tung and of "Marshal" Tito and *tutti quanti* gives us every day new evidence of the truth that democracy is not workable without foundations in the spiritual objectives set before us by Christ. In a recent issue of *The Commonweal*, Jacques Maritain writing on what he calls the *Problem of Means,* that is, the philosophical structure of political life, remarks:

> To try to reduce democracy to technocracy, and to expel from it the Gospel inspiration together with all faith in the supra-material, supra-mathematical, and supra-sensory realities, would be to try to deprive it of its very blood. Democracy can only live on Gospel inspiration.

The concern of a democratic society for the dignity of every man, for his rights, for his freedom to pursue his destiny, for the inviolability of his personality and his property, makes sense only when it reflects the higher preoccupation of Jesus Christ with "the least of these my brethren." The "Gospel inspiration" is not a vague, watery program of do-goodism. The Gospel inspiration is an acknowledgment of the real meaning and purpose of human life, an heroic confronting of the life of all of us, its exasperating limitations and its tremendous possibilities in the realm of the spirit.

The hidden inner mainspring of an effective democracy, then, lies in the sense of responsibility of its members. To operate as it should operate any society requires the constant care and watchfulness of those who govern it. Now, a democratic society is governed, or ought to be governed, by all its members. Therefore a democratic society demands a high degree of civic conscience and vigilance from all who participate in it.

Did you ever stop to reflect on the sum total of care and devotion that makes any community run smoothly? Looking about us at the great complex societies in which we live, we might easily get the impression that they operate automatically, as it were, that they run along in their traditional grooves on the force of momentum. This, I do believe, is a complete illusion. The communities of which we are a part and of which we are all too inclined to take the incalculable everyday services entirely for granted, continue to function as we expect them to function only because constantly, day and night, without a moment's interruption, other human beings are attentive to the machinery which makes them run. We have all probably experienced at one time or another the effects of minor or partial breakdowns in the mechanisms of our communities: an interruption in the electric current, a transportation strike, a blizzard overwhelming a city's street-clearing facilities. All these things are an indication of the extent to which we are dependent on the unsleeping vigilance of those who are charged with the operation of our society.

I should like to tell you something of a sinister experience involving the total suspension of all the operating forces in a vast human community. The net result of this suspension was not, mercifully, the complete destruction of the community concerned as might logically have been expected. But the brief vision of a great city without direction and without guidance gave me a frightening sense of the importance of responsibility in the conduct of human affairs.

A little of the history going before the circumstances I want to describe to you is needed to see the picture as it appeared to me. Throughout the winter of 1939-1940, a baffled Europe had been sitting out the months of the "phoney war", longing for something to happen and at the same time dreading what might happen. The fate of all of us seemed to hang on the unguessable fantasy of the sphinx of Berchtesgaden—what would Hitler finally do? The suspense was agonizing, intolerable. Then suddenly something did happen, everything seemed to happen at once.

In early May 1940 the German military machine overnight went into high gear. It was as though an abrupt tropical sun were turned on an ice field—the thaw was instantaneous and the flood of war was on. In a matter of days, one might almost say of hours, the neutral countries, Belgium, Luxemburg, the Netherlands, were invaded, overwhelmed, silenced. The north of France, pierced at innumerable points by the lightning thrusts of German armored columns, in no time became a seething mass of armed struggle. The strange, syncopated weeks flashed by as we sat in Paris with the torrent of war rushing in our direction.

40

The German forces bolted across France to the English Channel. In what by some incomprehensible magic of Mr. Churchill and the legerdemain of British propaganda has even up to this day been represented to the world as an heroic feat, Great Britain, with the aid of the bewildered French, withdrew her last armed man from the fight and retreated to the tremulous security of her island. France was left with only heartening words of encouragement.

The military situation became chaotic. The war communiqués published in the Paris press reflected the complete abandonment of the discipline of pretense; they dropped the high-flown jargon about strategic withdrawals and the shortening of lines of communication. The official communiqués acknowledged the existence of a situation best described by the phrase: *sauve qui peut!* every man for himself.

During all this time a stream of refugees poured into Paris through her northern approaches. The composition of this flock of terrorized human beings was a kind of barometer of the German advance—first Dutchmen and Belgians, then Frenchmen from the invaded north, and in a crescendo movement of panic, whole populations from regions increasingly near to the Capital, mixed finally with a sprinkling of fleeing soldiers, haggard, unkempt, utterly demoralized, a tragic indication of the extent of the military disaster. These people did not remain in Paris. They moved in a steady, distressing column through the northern approaches, traversed the city higgledy-piggledy, and went out through the southern gates. They stayed long enough only to swell the volume of rumors of despair, to contribute by their mute testimony to the anxiety, the confusion, finally the headlong panic of the population of the Capital. They blocked the roads from the north to all possibility of an orderly retreat by the French armies, choked the routes to the south with their indescribable cavalcade of cars and trucks and horses and household possessions and bicycles and baby carriages and pedestrians crippled with walking. They had no destination. They had not thought where they were going. They were only running away, impelled by a nameless and thoughtless and formless fear.

41

All this formed the background to what I want to tell you about, the strangest few days I have ever lived through. The experience of a great social organization, one of the world's greatest cities, suddenly and momentarily without structure, without direction, without guidance, a vast complex body left as it were with no brain to govern it.

In the last days of the military debacle, with the victorious German armies just over the horizon to the north and the east and the west, the French government summoned up a great blustering demonstration of verbal courage and announced that Paris would be defended, street by street, house by house, stone by stone. The inhabitants were exhorted to resist to the end, to spare no drop of their blood in the defense of the Fatherland, and to perish if need be in the smoking ruins of the City of Light rather than give in to the barbarian hordes which threatened them. Having terrified the population with these words of doom, the government then quietly departed out of the city and fled to the south. The cabinet left, the ministries left, the parliament left, the municipality of Paris left. The city was abandoned like a rudderless ship to fend for itself. Then began the brief duration of the strange interlude of which I want to convey an idea to you.

One by one, like lights going out in a village distant in the night, the functions and agencies of normal city life disappeared. Shops closed, traffic melted away out of the streets, the subway stopped running, most of the busses had gone out of the city to transport troops or refugees in futile directions. Only a few lonely taxis prowled about and a few intrepid bicycles. Movement ceased almost altogether.

Externally, save for this unnatural quiet, Paris was the unchanged beauty which has seduced the hearts of men throughout the world. The weather outdid itself in perfection. The lovely gold of early summer days flooded every corner of the city, contrasting the fresh green of her chestnut trees with the mellow tones of her ancient buildings and the reflected blue of her unspotted sky smiling up from the broad mirror of the Seine. And all of this beauty served only to intensify for me the feeling of terror inspired by this magnificent body without any soul. In all this great complex organism there was no pulsation save only the separate beatings of individual hearts constricted by the

42

doom which seemed to hang over them. More than half the population of Paris is said to have fled from the city by this time, but that still left some two million human beings to share a community out of which purpose, direction and coordination had been removed. It was, as it were, a de-socialized society, an agglomeration of people from which had been taken the cohesion infused by the principle of order and organization. The life of the city was without the guidance of authority, without law to which any sanction attached. The city vegetated on its own instincts.

On the first day of this curious interregnum I went across the city on foot with a friend who was interested even yet in leaving if this was possible, to investigate a rumor that trains were still running out of Paris from the *Gare d'Orléans*. We moved through a desert. Blinds and shutters were drawn everywhere. Life was quasi-invisible. Here and there a few neighbouring *concierges* were huddled in doorways, exchanging fantastic rumors in furtive whispers. At the station there was a wistful gathering of people come like ourselves to investigate the implausible report of a means of escape. Two young policemen stood at the main entrance to the station, answered the endless questions of the crowd as cheerfully as they could, gave a false semblance of stability and normalcy to the abandoned city. These two policemen were among the very few members of the Paris police who had failed to comply with the incomprehensible order to evacuate the city given to the police at the last minute by the departing government. They told me that they were without instructions and without superiors. They continued to function out of a kind of habit of duty, going about the city more for the reassurance their presence could give to the remaining population than out of a feeling that they could do any effective service.

The other days of this interlude deepened the impression of detachment given by this first one. An ancient bicycle was loaned to me by a friendly *concierge* and I went all about the city, looking for friends, observing the devastation wrought by silence and disorganization. Of the things to which one is accustomed in a great city, only two seemed to function as though life were normal: the telephone and the Mass. But for the most part, the numbers I dialed on the telephone produced only a mournful, unanswered ringing

43

in deserted apartments, and at Mass there was only a hand-
ful of those ageless women in black for whom, as they took
notice of the world, the passing confusion had no meaning.

There were notes of sardonic humor even in this atmosphere of tragedy. In all the quarters of the city through
which I wandered during those days, I observed only one
shop which never closed its doors—a taxidermist's establish-
ment in the Boulevard St. Germain. All else failing, even
in the face of incalculable disaster, not for one moment were
the people of Paris deprived of access to an abundant supply
of stuffed birds and animals!

On the third day a dense black pall moved in over the
city, hid the brilliant June sun from our view, settled upon
us in a fine soot, filtered everywhere until the whole city
and its remaining inhabitants were black with grime. We
learned afterwards that this visitation was caused by the
burning of immense supplies of petroleum further down
the river to the west of Paris. But as this mysterious cloud
settled, unexplained, upon us, it seemed as though heaven
itself had joined in the movement to overwhelm the city.
Towards evening rain began to fall, streaking down through
this veil of soot, descending upon us in swollen black drops.
As the night grew deeper, quite suddenly the rumbling of
artillery fire, which had been a constant accompaniment to
these strange days, ceased altogether. A padded, ominous
silence settled over the city.

During that night, without any fanfare, the German
forces moved into the city. The returning sun on the following morning picked out the brilliant red, white and
black of the swastika banners which floated languidly from
the Arch of Triumph and all the monuments of Paris. The
interregnum was over. Ironically, order and organization
moved back into the city to the disciplined tread of the
invaders' boots.

For a very long time now we have been considering
theories and events which may seem remote from our everyday lives and interests. What does all this have to do with
us, here and now? This much clearly, I do believe: That
the ideal structure of democracy cannot stand without us.
Our belief and our practice are the only supports upon
which it can be preserved. The concept of the equality of

all men will remain a mere notion until we bring it down out of the clouds of theory and put it into practice in every action of our lives. Human rights are nothing more than a subject for philosophical speculation unless we are willing to assert them actively for ourselves and all our fellow men. We are responsible for these things and the government we shall have to protect our rights and to make us equal in fact as well as in theory will be only a reflection of our active participation in its selection and support.

The American people today are divided, *grosso modo,* into three categories: Those who hold to democracy and are aware of its responsibilities. Those who follow the new anti-democratic doctrine of *hombre masa,* and they are an infinitesimal but active and articulate minority. Those who never think about these matters, and they are, probably, the vast majority of our fellow citizens. I put it to you that with the struggle engaged as it is for the survival of one or the other of these mutually exclusive doctrines: our American concept of democracy, and the totalitarian doctrine of *hombre masa,* there is no room for this third category, those who do not think about these matters. They must enlist under one or the other of the two conflicting banners. They can, of their free will, take the side of democracy and their added strength will win the day overwhelmingly for the cause of man. If they do not do this, they shall, whether they will it or not, find themselves brigaded in the ranks of totalitarianism and the case of man is lost, for who knows how long!

There are thinkers today as in other days who argue that the salvation of our society and our civilization must be sought in the creation of an *élite* of leaders, capable of thinking for the unthinking masses. Only such an *élite,* sensitive to the values of culture which are the substructure of our civilization, can see the way clearly to the preservation of these values. Thus speak earnest and thoughtful men like Thomas Stearns Elliott and George Santayana.

I do not believe that such an aristocratic solution is possible in the logic of a democratic society. In a book brought out a year ago under the auspices of the Kerby Foundation, *Introduction to Social Living,* Dr. William J. Kerby says:

45

The assumption that it is the chief duty of education to prepare leaders has so far prevailed as to have hidden from view the higher duty of preparing good followers. Only a socially-minded citizenry can so discipline leadership as to make it safe for democracy. An indifferent citizenry neither produces nor supports socially-minded leaders.

For a society irrevocably committed to the belief that all men are created equal, salvation could not possibly be found in a course consisting, ultimately, in building up a structure of human inequality, of developing the inequalities which, in nature, exist among men. The salvation for our society, I am convinced, must be sought in the literal meaning of our fundamental belief in human equality and human rights and in the real application of this belief to our world.

Religion and the Practice of the Law

REV. FRANCIS J. POWERS, C.S.V., S.J.D.
Instructor in Politics
The Catholic University of America

I.

Religion does have relevancy to law. Religion is a basic component of our legal blood stream. Its influence permeates the whole field of the law. The great concepts which form the framework of our law, both public and private, are essentially religious. Religious and moral ideas and ideals constitute the very soul of our legal inheritance.

Basically, our law rests on a true concept of man as a being possessed of reason, will and a spiritual nature. Our legal traditions are based upon a recognition of the dignity of human life and of those freedoms and liberties which enhance and enrich it. Our law demands respect for life and for the liberty without which it would be spiritually and socially meaningless. The law offers broad protection for those objects which are regarded as immediate extensions of the human personality. It demands respect for property which it views as an institution intrinsically related to the human personality and its fulfillment. Acknowledging man's social nature, our laws have traditionally protected rights of association and communication of ideas. It recognizes that man has spiritual relationships and it respects his conscience.

The very Constitution of this nation is not without religious inspiration. Implicit in it is a recognition of the philosophical truth that the State, whose proper object is the securing of the common temporal good, is limited by the inalienable rights of the human personality. The idea of legal limitation of governmental action, of legal responsibility for official action and the securing of the rights of individuals against arbitrary governmental conduct is the essence of constitutionalism. It is postulated on the concept of the primacy of the individual and the supremacy of reason over force. It is a reflection of the natural law.[1]

[1] For a brief but excellent treatment of this point see Edward S. Corwin, "Debt of American Constitutional Law to Natural Law Concepts", 25 *Notre Dame Lawyer* 258-84 (1950).

The spirit of our fundamental law is opposed to the deposit of unlimited governmental power anywhere. The Fifth and Fourteenth Amendments seek to secure life, liberty and property against arbitrary or unreasonable governmental action. The Constitution seeks to protect the person against summary detention without cause, to protect the home against unwarranted governmental invasion and to safeguard the great spiritual freedoms of speech, press, religion and assembly. The principles of separation of powers, judicial review, due process, equal protection and the provisions of the Constitution relating to *habeas corpus,* search and seizure and civil liberties are rooted in the natural law. It is in its implications a deeply spiritual document.

Religiously inspired ideas also pervade our governmental and legal institutions. Ours is a government of laws. Our constitutions and legislative measures have been enacted through a representative process based on the rationality and freedom of man and upon the assumption that men know right from wrong and will strive earnestly for what is right. The judicial process is given substance and sanction by religion.

Our entire system of judicial administration has for its ultimate object the attainment of justice. And the concept of justice is basically religious. Stated simply, justice is a moral virtue which disposes and moves one to respect the rights of others. It is a constant and permanent determination of the will to render to each man that which is his due. It is fundamentally religious and a condition precedent to its existence is a recognition by one man, or by men in association, of the essential spiritual dignity and equality of human nature in their fellow men. Rights and duties, with which the law is much concerned, grow out of this recognition.

Currently, our legislators and courts are concerned with civil liberties, with the basic rights and immunities of the individual. A proper solution to any problem in this area must take into account the fact that these rights and freedoms are rooted in the spiritual. These rights are part and parcel of man's moral endowment. They are claims or demands of the human personality, part of human nature, and hence inalienable. Liberty is simply the freedom to exer-

48

cise these rights within the orbit set by reason and just law. Rights and liberties are not ends in themselves but are means to an end, namely, the fulfillment of one's nature. Rights and liberties can have substance and meaning only so long as they are associated with the spiritual nature of man. This is the only sound basis for determining either their extension or limitation.

Religion and morality give to law its ultimate sanction. And our legal system badly is in need of high moral inspiration and sanction. Judicial administration is seriously handicapped by unconscionable conduct by litigants and advocates alike. This is no idle charge. Jurists in increasing numbers are warning us that the entire judicial process is being undermined seriously by perjury on the part of parties and witnesses and the subornation of perjury by lawyers. The sanctity of the oath is vital to the administration of justice. Fear of the penalties of perjury is an inadequate sanction to preserve the integrity of the judicial process.

II.

Roscoe Pound, foremost American scholar in the realm of jurisprudence, has traced brilliantly the powerful and beneficent influence of religion in the development of the ideas of universality, authority, good faith and the 'higher law' concept in law.[2] These postulates, declared the Dean, form the basis of the modern civil and common law systems. A brief examination of the three last mentioned postulates appears particularly timely.

Authority, as a religiously inspired concept, has long been a keystone of the law. In the beginning of law in the modern world, Pound said, the Church taught and lawyers learned from her, and we have since assumed, that what lay behind law in all its meanings was the concept of authority. Religion teaches that authority is not simply or even essentially coercion and that its purpose is more than the erection of a protective system. In origin it is a consequence of the social nature of man and is therefore of mediate divine origin. Its primary function is to govern and to direct. Saint Thomas wrote that to govern means to bring the thing

---

[2] Roscoe Pound, "The Church in Legal History", in *Jubilee Law Lectures*, Washington: Catholic University Press, 1939, pp. 3-97. This was a series of four lectures delivered at the Catholic University.

49

governed in a suitable way to its proper end. Authority, therefore, is chiefly directive. Moreover, it is a unitive principle. Men in society are pursuing a common temporal end and they should orient their activities toward this end. If the ends of society were always clearly defined and readily evident and the means necessary for their attainment perfectly outlined, and all men cooperated harmoniously in the accomplishing of these purposes, there would be no need for authority. But such is not the case. Frequently the end is imperfectly perceived and the most suitable means to attain it, once it is perceived, are not readily evident. Hence, the need for a unifying directive force. The real sanction of authority is the voice of reason. Force is an incident of sanction but authority is much more than force. Authority is the source of social order, social unity, social action and is a necessity in social life. Such is the traditional scholastic concept of authority which has come down to us as a received ideal in the law.[3]

Today, Pound declared, this concept has been discarded in many quarters. The psychological realists tell us that all that is behind law is a fatherly complex satisfying the innate cravings of men to be led by the hand as they were when they were children. The skeptical realists, and their names are legion, hold that the only authority behind law is threats and execution of threats by those who wield political power in society. Law is nothing more than the command of the sovereign State.[4]

Pius XII has been greatly concerned with the rise of a juridical positivism which bases the authority behind law on the naked power of the State independent of any other consideration. This is not to say that advocates of this theory are depraved or brutal men who approve of State excesses. They even talk of morality and its place in social life. Morality should influence the formulation of law. But once enacted or declared as law by the supreme authority of the State it may not be questioned, they say, on grounds of morality and no citizen has the right to be ex-

---

[3] See Yves Simon, "Nature and Function of Authority", *Aquinas Lecture,* Milwaukee: Marquette University Press, 1940.

[4] For a comprehensive bibliography on legal realism see E. N. Garlan, *Legal Realism and Justice,* New York: Columbia University Press, 1941. For a very brief summary and appraisal of realist views see the present writer's *Religious Liberty and the Police Power of the State,* Washington: Catholic University Press, 1948, pp. 20-26.

cused from executing or applying it. Juridical positivism disassociates law from dependence upon or conformity with any order transcending the human legislator. It invests the State with an absolute control over the citizen by endowing it with uncontrolled and therefore irresponsible power. The implications of this doctrine on the lawyer, judge and public official are perfectly obvious.

In *Summi Pontificatus*,[5] his first Encyclical, Pius XII spoke of the error of those who "seek to dispense the civil authority from observing any of those higher laws which have their origin in God." The 1942 Christmas Message[6] of Pius condemned the false postulate of juridical positivism which "attributes a deceptive majesty to the setting up of purely human laws and which leaves the way open for a fatal divorce of law from morality . . . " In the same message he called for a constitutionalism which "gives man a right to juridical security, and accordingly grants him a sphere of rights immune from all arbitrary attacks." Speaking to the Union of Italian Catholic Jurists in November of 1949 the Pontiff treated the subject of juridical positivism in detail and set forth a series of norms to be followed by jurists when confronted with it in practice.[7] It is clear, Pius said, that the jurist cannot acquire a social concept of law and cannot formulate a science of jurisprudence unless man is viewed as a spiritual being. The nature of law cannot be derived except from the nature of man, the Pontiff insisted, and the concept of authority which gives vitality, measure and sanction to law is intrinsically related to that nature. It follows, then, that each lawyer must look beyond human law.

Pius XII and Dean Pound are as one in warning that the cult of stark force unrelated to reason or the nature of man and unrestrained by reference to any transcendent order is becoming the new authority behind positive law.

---

[5] Pius XII, *Summi Pontificatus*, on "The Function of the State in the Modern World", in *Principles For Peace* (Koenig, ed.), Washington: National Catholic Welfare Conference, 1943, pp. 592-615.

[6] Pius XII, 1942 Christmas Message, English translation in *Principles for Peace*, pp. 789-806.

[7] Pius XII, Allocution, to Union of Italian Catholic Jurists, November 6, 1949, English translation in *Catholic Mind*, XLVIII (January, 1950), 53-58.

III.

Good faith, Pound declared in the Jubilee Lectures, is a fundamental religious conception and no less a fundamental legal conception. Good faith is the substance around which much of our law of trusts, equity, uses, mortgages and restitution is built. It is discernible, too, in other areas of law.

From the twelfth to the seventeenth centuries the principle of good faith had behind it the direct and powerful force of the Church. Civil obligation arose from a promise, from consent, because of the religious implications present. The effect of the promissory oath on our law is immeasurable. In the ages when religion was the predominant force in society a man who did not keep his promise committed a sin and incurred ecclesiastical penalties. Fulfillment and performance of promises and agreements were exacted of the Christian by ecclesiastical courts on the basis of religious obligation without reference to the requirements of legal formality.

The great historians of the Common Law tell us that throughout the Middle Ages the Court of Chancery, composed very largely of clerics and canonists, was the center of the legal system and the political center of the Constitution. The Chancery Courts exercised considerable supervision over the administration of justice in all the King's Courts and granted equitable relief and remedies in instances where in the judgment of the Chancellor the King's Courts, the law courts, had failed to do justice. The Chancery Courts also had jurisdiction over clerics and laymen in ecclesiastical matters, in matrimonial affairs, wills, usury, defamation and in matters of breaches of faith. During all the creative centuries of the Common Law, Richard O'Sullivan writes, the end of the law was a moral end and for all the great lawyers from Bracton to Mansfield jurisprudence was related to religion and ethics.[8] The lustre of the glorious centuries of the Common Law under the inspiration of the moral force of religion has dimmed in the intervening ages—but it is not entirely extinguished in our legal order today.

Predictability in human affairs is an important value in law and in civilization. In a memorable passage in legal

---

[8] Richard O'Sullivan, "Christian Philosophy in the Common Law", *Aquinas Papers*, No. 6, Westminster: The Newman Press, 1947.

literature Pound wrote that the ability of men to act with assurance in reliance upon the word of fellow men is one of the roots of all human progress. An unprincipled man is one who will not or who may not act according to the norms of moral predictability, he may or he may not keep his word. He is untrustworthy and confidence cannot be reposed in his promises. For the good of the social order, he may have to be coerced into keeping his promises. Law is one of the agencies of such coercion. But the Dean pointed out that law as an instrument of social control has its limitations in this area and that it cannot in fact accomplish the end desired. Religion, morals and law stand behind civilization in maintaining the integrity and predicability in human conduct without which a well ordered social order is impossible. Today, the burden, almost in its entirety, has been shifted to the law. A secularized age has imposed on law a function more proper to religion. The sanction of law now rests on force or on a naive trust in public education rather than on religion. Confidence in the new sanction is misplaced, said the Dean, for the appeal to the secularized conscience "has neither the power of impressing moral precepts which was exerted by the home nor the intelligent organized power of direction and coercion exerted by the Church." The confusion and bewilderment as to the real foundations of the legal order and the decline of the religiously inspired concept of good faith in juristic thought has placed the legal order under a heavy burden.

IV.

Constitutionalism is in essence a spiritual concept. McIlwain is authority for the proposition that in all its successive stages of development, constitutionalism has one essential quality; it is a legal limitation on government and arbitrary rule for the purpose of securing the basic rights of the individual.[9] In a sentence that has stirred the soul of men down through the centuries, Bracton pronounced the great constitutional principle: "The King is under God and the law." The King is under God and the law; he is bound by the eternal law of God, by the law of reason—the natural

---

[9] C. H. McIlwain, *Constitutionalism, Ancient and Modern* (rev. ed.), Ithaca: Cornell University Press, 1947. This is an unexcelled brief treatment of the development of the idea of constitutionalism.

law—and by the law of the land. English jurisprudence of the Medieval period saw in law this threefold order.

Constitutionalism is far from a purely negative concept of restraint. It has positive connotations. It indirectly gave rise to the legally free but responsible man of the Common Law. Under the influence of Christian thought every man was regarded by the law as morally and intellectually autonomous and the source of rational action. The natural law demands freedom for the individual in the fulfillment of his personality. Inspired by Christian natural law ideas the Common Law freed men from the legal bonds of serfdom and slavery. To acknowledge that a man was spiritual was to recognize him as free. But if man was rational and free he was also accountable for the use of his freedom. He is answerable for his acts and omissions. On this rational basis has been built much of our law of torts and crime.

The Christian sense of personal freedom and responsibility became the animating principle of the Common Law and wrought a social revolution in England. The free and responsible man became an institution and that institution has come down to us as a sacred heritage.

But the slow decline of the spiritual ideal and religion in social life brought with it a corresponding change in the schools of jurisprudence. In time the teaching of Machiavelli in "The Prince" on the alleged distinction between public and private morality came to prevail and the idea of juridical positivism arose in one form or another to wage war with the Christian concept of constitutionalism.

In the area of public law, particularly constitutional law, juridical positivism is the culmination of the process of deleting religion and spiritual values from the law. Speaking to the members of the Roman Rota in 1949 Pius XII dwelt at length on the devastating influence of juridical positivism on the concept of constitutionalism. Stressing the dangers inherent in the tendency of modern States to pervert law into an instrument of policy for the accomplishing of purely political and administrative ends, Pius pointed out that everything which is done or ordered to be done officially is not necessarily true law. "The mere fact", he stated, "of a law being declared by the legislative power as an obligatory norm in the State, this fact, alone and by itself, is not enough to create true law." The belief that everything that is done officially is real law is "an error which is at the basis of State absolutism and which is equivalent to a deification of the State itself." The principle of constitutionalism has vitality only when law restrains arbitrary State action; when arbitrary State action determines what is law constitutionalism is dead.

Pius has been greatly concerned with the moral problem, the question of conscience, which juridical positivism poses in the execution of an unjust law by judges and public officials. May officials cast the burden of responsibility on those who enacted or decreed the measure and proceed to carry it into force or act under it with moral impunity? Is the defense of reliance upon superior command or authority morally and legally acceptable? These are far from simply theoretical questions. The Pontiff noted that the world has recently witnessed and is still experiencing the terrible state to which judges and public officials may be reduced, morally, under the dominance of juridical positivism. The conflict between conscience and unjust law has now reached a critical stage. The defense of reliance on superior command in the execution of unjust law, the Pope also noted, was rejected by the conscience of the civilized world at Nuremberg.[10]

V.

During the creative era of our law jurisprudence was oriented toward God. The ends of the law were measured in terms of religion and spiritual values. The limits of law were gauged in terms of the law of God and the nature of man. In contemporary jurisprudence God, religion and spiritual values are treated frequently as irrelevant factors. The current attitude is typified, I believe, by the statement of Jerome Frank in his well-known "Law and the Modern Mind" that: "The close and avowed relation of law to religion is a matter of the distant past". "The legal pro-

---

[10] Pius XII recently considered the matter of Juridical positivism in the above-mentioned Allocution to the Roman Rota, November 13, 1949, French translation in *Documentation Catholique*, 1949, 1543-8; also in an Allocution to the International Congress of Private Law, July 15, 1950, English translation in *Catholic Mind*, XLVIII (December, 1950), 754-56; and in an Allocution to the International Convention of the Catholic Press, February 18, 1950, English trnslation in *Catholic Mind*, XLVIII (December, 1950), 749-54. For a good commentary on the point see J. Sander, S.J., "Juridical Positivism", *The Clergy Monthly*, XIV (November, 1950) 365-374. B. F. Brown and J. B. Keenan, *Crimes Against International Law*, Washington: Public Affairs Press, 1950, is a brilliant treatise on the application of natural law concepts to the punishing of aggressive warfare and crimes against international law.

fession", he continued, "has long since been split off from the priesthood." It would be idle to deny that this statement is not without considerable factual basis.

Addressing groups of jurists recently, Pius XII presented inspiring descriptions of jurisprudence ennobled by religion and of the role of a true Catholic jurist in the pursuit of his calling. Borrowing the words of the third-century jurist Ulpian, the Pontiff described jurisprudence as: "The knowledge of things human and divine, the science of right and wrong."[11] After noting the noble objective assigned to juridical science, the pursuit of justice, Pius spoke of the need of spiritual vision for the true lawyer. A jurist worthy of the name, he said, must above all have knowledge of divine things because without this higher knowledge the human panorama with which the lawyer deals would not have complete meaning: "The jurist . . . in the exercise of his profession moves between the finite and the Infinite, between the divine and the human, and in this necessary movement lies the nobility of the science he cultivates."[12] Human affairs, with which the lawyer deals, are so intimately entwined with the divine that they cannot be understood completely without reference to God. True, the lawyer is not called to theological speculation, but, Pius said, "if he is incapable of rising to the highest transcendent Reality, from whose will the order of the visible universe and . . . the human race with its inherent and necessary laws is derived, it will be impossible for him to perceive in all its marvellous unity and its intimate spiritual depths the interlacing of social relations and their regulative norms over which the law presides."[13] The law, said Pius, should lead to God. From God it receives light and clearness, vigor and strength, meaning and content.

Arnold Toynbee in "Civilization on Trial" wrote that Western civilization is now living on the spiritual capital of the past and that such capital faces depletion unless quickly replenished. This generalization might well be applied to law and jurisprudence. The process of renewing the spiritual content of our law and reorienting it toward God presents a formidable but glorious challenge to those who pursue a legal calling.

---

[11] Allocution to the Union of Italian Catholic Jurists, *op. cit.*, 54-55.
[12] *Ibid.*, 56.
[13] *Ibid.*, 55.

The Lawyer and Mental Health

REV. JAMES VAN DER VELDT, O.F.M., Ph. D.
Associate Professor of Psychology
The Catholic University of America

We witness at the present time an ever growing interest
in the problem of mental health. We have national and
international congresses in which psychologists, psychiatrists, sociologists, anthropologists and plain ordinary people without any "ist" behind their names join hands to
view the problem from all angles. As a matter of fact the
next international congress on mental health will convene
at Mexico City in December of this year. I attended the last
meeting of the National Association for Mental Health held
in New York on November 16 and 17, 1950 and I was
impressed by the earnestness with which the members of
the convention approached the problem. All of those interested in mental health are strongly convinced that there
is something rotten not only in the State of Denmark but in
the state of the whole world and are earnestly striving not
only to rebuild our present world but to build a better one.

I have the greatest respect for the serious efforts of these
architects but I am somewhat flabbergasted by the variety
of suggestions proposed to achieve that purpose. Some see
the solution in preventive child psychiatry, others in prop-
agating the principles of democracy, still others feel that
world citizenship should be our goal and so we could
continue.

There is one feature in many of these attempts to im-
prove the condition of our society which might strike many
an onlooker. Until recently little or no attention was paid
to the religious and moral aspects of the mental health of
our society. For many decades, in fact, for more than a
century, most systems of sociology, psychology, politics,
economics, have severed all relationship with morality. The
proponents of those sciences profess not only not to be concerned with the moral acceptability of people's behavior,
but they believe that they *should* not be concerned with
moral problems on penalty of ceasing to be scientific.

57

Hence, they have banished from their field of interest the very reference not only of religious but also of sound moral principles.

Of late, however, a change has become noticeable; we seem to witness a turning of the tide inasmuch as some of those, interested in the people's mental health, are turning their attention to religious and moral factors. Serious people have begun to think about the reasons of the catastrophic condition of our crumbling society: a few strikes every day, a bloody revolution somewhere every half year and a bloodier world war every twenty years, have made them ask the question, if the mental confusion in the world is not in final analysis a moral problem. And ever more people seem willing to agree that the problem of rebuilding our present world on a sounder basis involves the re-establishment of moral principles and ideals.

Obviously the rebuilding of our disorganized world can be achieved only through the restoration of the mental health of the individuals who make up the world. Hence a growing number of those who are interested in restoring the people's mental health feel that they should also concern themselves with the problem of how to teach the people moral values. In this respect I wish to quote the British psychiatrist, J. C. Flugel, who writes: "It is pretty generally agreed that the problem of rebuilding our tottering society upon a sounder basis is *to some extent* a moral problem."[1] "To some extent", seems to be one of those typically British understatements. We prefer to say, to a very large extent.

Anyway, it is gratifying to see that people begin to realize that the restoration of mental health needs the aid of moral principles. The current trend is definitely in that direction as may be gleaned from several recent publications on mental health and religion, mental health and morals. (*Peace of Soul, Society and Morals, etc.*) The Swiss psychiatrist, Jung, more than twenty years ago, said that he would have few patients, if people lived up to the moral teachings of their religion. And we find an echo of that statement in the opinion of many a modern psychiatrist. This recent interest in moral problems is definitely agreeable. But, here

---

[1] J. C. Flugel, *Man, Morals and Society,* New York, International University Press, 1945, p. 9.

we run into difficulties. Where shall we find the moral principles and ideals that will help to make people recover their mental health, once they have lost it, or to prevent them from becoming mentally ill?

Many people believe that the ultimate and stable principles of morality should be established by psychology, psychiatry, sociology, anthropology or any such science or by the concerted effort of all of them. But this is a very serious mistake, because any system based exclusively upon the findings of science is necessarily man-made and has therefore only a relative value.

We, as Catholics, hold that there is an absolute objective norm of morality. By this we mean that God has laid down a set of rules which form the standard by which a person's actions must be judged as either morally right or morally wrong. God made his eternal law known to man by endowing him with a rational nature. Because man is able to discover and to understand the main obligations of God's law through his rational nature, we speak of the natural law. Besides, God, in his mercy, revealed his will through positive revelation. This positive divine law was promulgated twice in history, once as the old law, including the Ten Commandments, through Moses, and once more through Jesus Christ, the Son of God, as the law of the New Testament.

I felt it necessary to present to you this brief outline of our system of morality, because here we meet the demarcation line which separates our system from all other moral systems. Anyone who denies the existence of an ultimate objective norm, to be found in the mind of the Creator, is bound to look somewhere else in order to find a basis for the moral order. He may try to locate the source of morality in society, tradition, customs, the State, or dictators, but all such theories proclaim in final analysis that the moral order is manmade, and anyone who accepts such a theory, undermines moral stability. I am not going to bother you with a refutation of the relativistic theories of morality, but I wish to draw your attention to the fact that, if one refuses to admit absolute God-given ethical standards, he may construct the most ingenious theories; but, when put to the test, they all fall to pieces. A simple example may clarify this statement. When Hitler and his abettors exterminated thousands of Jews by locking them up in gas chambers, and made soap out of the fat of their bodies and lamp shades out of their skins, was the act of those "supermen" right or wrong, good or bad? Everyone in his right mind will answer that it was evil. But why? Because it is inhuman! But why is it inhuman? The basic dogma of Naziism was the blood-and-soil dogma. Anything that was good and useful for the German race was considered morally good. Now, so the Nazis reasoned, the extermination of the Jews is good and beneficial to the German race; hence it is morally good. It would be difficult to find fault with this syllogism, once one accepts the major premise. Yet a great many people accept as the principle and basis of all morality just that very premise, that is, what is useful is morally good. But if they accept it, then they should also accept the logical consequences of this principle and—coming back to our example—feel no scruples at washing their faces with soap made of human fat.

One may object that our society does not tolerate such an interpretation. Indeed, our society does perhaps condemn such things. But why should our society be the measuring-stick of good and evil? In the East, a society is being formed in which many things that we call evil are considered desirable, and vice versa. If society is its own moral standard, why are the concepts of our society superior to those of the other one? If our concepts of good and evil have only a relative value, they may come some day to mean the very reverse of what we mean by them at present. Perhaps the present man will some day change into the superman of Nietzsche, who preached the transformation of all values, and to whom mercy, loyalty and fairness were immoral weaknesses, and hatred, sin and pride, moral greatnesses. We have not reached that stage of evolution yet, and hatred, sin and pride still make neurotics out of many people, including Nietzsche.

Listen to the following excerpt taken from Nietzsche's *Zarathustra*. "Evil is the greatest power in man. Man must become better by becoming more wicked,—that is what I teach. The greatest wickedness is necessary to make the best superman. . . . Yes, I teach you to become supermen! The superman gives meaning to the World. . . . At one time sin against God was considered the greatest sin. But

God has died and therefore there are no more sinners. . . . 'Nothing is true, everything is allowed', thus I said to myself. 'To live as I please or not to live at all', that is how I will it."

This is Nietzsche's message to the world: the devaluation of values. Yet these blasphemous rantings are the ultimate and logical consequence of man-made morality. And the result of such a morality is the precise opposite of mental health, the witness being Nietzsche himself, because he died in an insane asylum.

The only reasonable solution of the problem of morality is that no system of moral rules will stand the test unless it is based on objective and absolute principles. This is the Catholic position.

After having outlined our Catholic position concerning matters of morality, let us now return to the problem of mental health. We saw that ever more authors are prepared to accept the thesis that moral principles contribute to restore people's mental health. If we wish to help a psycho-neurotic, it is not enough to psychoanalyze him and leave him with his analysis, but we must educate him to become a morally responsible person who is willing to regulate his life according to moral principles. If we want to make a better man out of a criminal, it is not enough to punish him and send him to jail, but we must try to offer him a better plan of life for the future. If juvenile delinquency can be fought, it is not enough to subject the youngsters to a battery of psychological tests, but we have to develop the traces of moral goodness which are found in all of them. If an alcoholic can be helped at all, we may show him that his condition is the result of a distorted childhood, of "momism" (Strecker), an escape mechanism, and so on. And then what? An insight in the underlying causes of his urge does not reform the alcoholic. But alcoholics themselves confess that the acceptance of moral and religious motives greatly contributes to their staying sober. Take the case of a man who carries on an extra-marital affair and thus causes severe qualms of conscience in himself and brings untold grief upon his wife and family. Liebman in his book *Peace of Mind* tells us that the method of treatment consists solely in revealing to the man the causes of what Liebman euphemistically calls his "neurotic be-

61

havior",—causes which would be found in his childhood experiences, but that the man should in no way be "told what to do or how to act". This method—we are made to believe—would change the adulterer into an exemplary husband. It seems to me that one must be very naive if he accepts such a statement, and I can well understand that this book *Peace of Mind* which at one time was a best-seller, recently was called by one of Liebman's co-religionists an *absurd book.*[2] Nobody will convert an adulterer without moral motives, and age-old experience has taught us that no self-understanding will liberate a person from his sexual yearnings without self-control.

All this is, of course, quite evident to us, but—as I said— it took the official mental hygienists a long time before they were willing to admit the importance of moral principles. And now that they are willing to do so, we are faced with a very serious problem. Most of the present-day writers who advocate the importance of moral values for the preservation or restoration of people's mental health, believe in a humanistic, man-made norm of morality. In other words, they are standing at the other side of the demarcation line.

But we are again confronted with all the difficulties in herent in a man-made system of morality. Try to convince a criminal to behave and conduct a morally acceptable life. And as a motive you may tell him—as Durkheim would do —that society does not approve of his behavior. But the criminal hates society, because he blames it for his failure in life. As long as he fails to see that there is a law-giver superior to society, the moral norms of society won't make any impression on him. You may tell him—as Freud would suggest—to adopt the moral standards of his environment. But your criminal *has* adopted the moral standards of *his* environment, and they have landed him where he is, in jail. You may tell him that human destiny requires that he act as an honest man—as Erich Fromm would suggest, but your client might well ask: what is my destiny? What right do you have to determine my destiny? And unless you can point at the supreme law-giver who leads the destiny of all men, you would be hard pressed for a reasonable answer. You might, with Brock Chisholm, tell your client that our present standards of morality are too rigorous and that,

---

[2] David Daiches, in the February issue of *Commentary,* 1951.

because of their rigidity, they are the cause of your man's failures.[3] It would be indeed interesting to see your criminal's reaction to such a statement. In fact, if Chisholm's suggestion of what he calls superior ethics, is taken at its face value, the question may well be asked whether it does not lead eventually to Nietschze's superman and, therefore, also to Nietschze's paranoia.

These few examples show you that relativistic theories of morality, when tested in individual concrete cases, fail miserably. We all seem to agree that we need moral principles to put the world and the individuals in it on a solid footing, but man-made principles won't bring the solution, because they lack stability. Therefore, we come once more to the conclusion that only those standards of morality will help us, which are derived from the Eternal Lawgiver.

Supposing that we believe in objective, stable standards of morality, laid down in the natural law and the positive divine law, in other words in the Ten Commandments, we now ask: who is going to apply them to concrete cases, which treat of people whose mental and moral life is impaired?

There are the educators who can contribute immensely to the mental, emotional and moral well-being of the future generation, provided of course that they themselves possess correct moral concepts. In that respect I may refer to the complaint made by the psychologist Vernon Jones, who says that teachers have standards in spelling, but not always in morals.[4] I may, in parentheses, mention that I quoted Jones' statement in a paper which I read at the latest White House Conference. A few days later I received a letter from some gentleman in Buffalo in which he called me several unprintable names for having slurred the teachers' profession. Of course, the letter landed in the waste basket, because I had done nothing but quote a well-know psychologist.

Another group of men and women who can do an outstanding job in employing moral ideals for the betterment of our people's mental health are the psychiatrists, and we should add that our Catholic psychiatrists have achieved excellent results with their re-education method. There

---

[3] E. Brock Chisholm, *The Psychiatry of Enduring Peace and Social Progress*, William A. White Lectures, published by *Psychiatry*, 9 (1946).

[4] Vernon Jones, "Ideas on Right and Wrong Among Teachers and Children," Teacher's College Record, 30 (1929), 529-541.

are, furthermore, the priests. But they do not always have access to the mentally and morally derailed. There are the social workers, the nurses and many other professional people.

There are also the lawyers. They come in daily contact with a rather variegated sample of humanity: the criminals, the tramps, the alcoholics, the perverts, the juvenile delinquents, the candidates for divorce,—to mention but a small part of the endless litany of human wickedness and stupidity. Now, far be it from me to contend that the lawyer should set himself up as a peddler of morality, a schoolmaster or a preacher. Yet, it can hardly be denied that the lawyer, apart from his professional duties or rather on top of them, is in a unique position to help these people to become better men and women. In certain cases the education of these people apparently has failed; some may approach a psychiatrist, but not all, and far from all will feel inclined to see a priest. But all of them come in contact with the lawyer.

It is of course the lawyer's duty to defend the cause of his clients in court. When he has taken upon himself to defend a case, he may well find loopholes in the law which make it possible to plead for the freedom of his client. This is the legal aspect of the case, but that is by no means the whole story. Freedom from liability of punishment is not freedom from moral responsibility. Many a defendant who is freed in court, is not always free in the eyes of God. Although legally not liable to prosecution, he may well be morally reprehensible. There are—as we know—many lawyers who profess not to be interested in their client's moral responsibility, but there are, thanks be to God, also lawyers who endeavor to help their clients in their moral difficulties, knowing that in that manner they contribute to their mental and emotional happiness. They can perform this task not in court but in the office situation where they occupy the position of confidant and counselor.

To be sure, certain types of clients pretend not to feel any moral responsibility, like the cynics who contend that after all there is no difference between right and wrong. However, one should not accept such protestations too readily. When one probes a little deeper into the psyche of a person one practically always finds traces of conscience.

64

In this respect I wish to refer to the highly interesting work of the existential analysts who, although analysts, are very far removed from Freud's psychoanalysis. They maintain that existential analysis is able to discover moral and religious thoughts and values—even when treating people who are, or profess to be, entirely unconscious of such values. Even though these values are at times hidden deep in the person's unconscious, they hold that they can be brought to the surface. They also hold that people sometimes become mentally disturbed because they fail to realize, or have repressed these values within themselves. And they refuse to be deluded into the belief that man is a sublimated animal—as Freud would say—as long as they can prove that he hides within himself a repressed angel. Obviously a lawyer does not have at his disposal the techniques and devices which an analyst uses to bring to the fore these hidden moral forces in a person, but often enough he does not need these devices. A simple confidential heart-to-heart talk with his client may well suffice to make him re-discover his conscience.

I remember a case of a sailor of Polish ancestry. He had been educated in a Catholic orphanage and—as he told me —kept Father So-and-so, the chaplain of the institution, in respectful remembrance. After leaving the orphanage the turmoil of adolescence made him stay away from the Church, and going to sea did the rest. He had broken all the precepts of the Church as well as all the Commandments, except perhaps the fifth, forbidding murder. And he confided to me that in his opinion it made little difference what one did, because: "Who can tell what is good or evil?" Thereupon I asked him: would you honestly dare to express that same opinion to your old friend, Father So-and-so. And then he blurted out: "No, you are right; deep down in my heart there is something that calls me a scoundrel and I cannot get away from it."

An appeal to conscience will often prevent not only moral but also mental grief. And this is frequently so in divorce cases, particularly when both parties are Catholic. It is easy enough for a lawyer, especially in this country, to obtain a divorce in court. It suffices to stress the incompatibility of character, but is it not more important to stress the indissolubility of marriage? A divorce, apart from endangering the eternal salvation of those who seek it, also brings along very unhappy consequences. Every psychiatrist and social worker can tell you that the mental and emotional distress of the children brought to them is often due to broken homes. And, therefore, if a lawyer can reconcile husband and wife and make them obey the law of the Church, he prevents untold grief of both parents and children.

An excellent way for a lawyer to promote moral and mental health is sponsoring a delinquent, especially a juvenile delinquent. The relationship between a delinquent and his sponsor is basically very simple. Discussing this relationship, G. Howland Shaw, Chairman, Continuing Committee, National Conference on Prevention and Control of Juvenile Delinquency, Washington, D. C., has this to say: "In last analysis there is nothing complicated about sponsoring a juvenile delinquent. It is simply the art by which an adult works out a constructive relationship with a youngster who has been or who is in trouble, to the mutual benefit of both the youngster and the adult. It has been called 'the art of disinterested friendship' and that is exactly what it is. You, a normal and average adult, are put in touch by a competent authority with a youngster in some training school or reformatory. The two of you 'click', the boy likes you, you like the boy. You get to understand each other, a relationship develops which helps the boy to grow and helps you to grow, too. The relationship is continued after the boy leaves the institution, sometimes for many years."[5]

However, despite its basic simplicity, a sponsoring program requires certain conditions in order to be successful. In case the sponsor is a lawyer or any other non-professional counselor, he should be constantly aware of the fact that he is a layman from the point of view of the several disciplines which deal scientifically with human behavior. He, therefore, must seek professional guidance. With regard to this point I wish to quote again G. Howland Shaw: "To be sure, it is reasonable to expect that as time goes on he will acquire some degree of familiarity with professional terms

[5] G. Howland Shaw, "Sponsoring a Delinquent," Address delivered before the Thirty-Fourth Meeting of the National Conference of Catholic Charities, Boston, Mass., October 9-13, 1948; reprinted in *Federal Probation Quarterly*, December, 1948.

and literature, but even then he is a layman and any illusions to the contrary are certain to lead to serious consequences. The sponsor therefore must accept and seek professional guidance. The boy on placement or parole from a training school or reformatory has a social worker or a parole officer who is a professional and who is in official charge. The sponsor must co-operate fully and at all times with this social worker or parole officer. Indeed, the willingness to accept and the desire to profit from professional guidance are important guarantees of the sponsor's seriousness and competence."

I mentioned a few instances in which a lawyer may promote the moral and mental health of our people. If a lawyer tries to make better men and women of his clients by bolstering the voice of conscience and by making them accept or re-accept the principles of the moral law, he contributes greatly to their mental health and happiness. And when a lawyer tries to re-awaken moral values in the heart of his client, what else does he do but re-establish the natural and positive divine law? True, he must take up the legal defense of his clients, but at the same time he should also defend the rights of the divine Lawgiver.

In doing so he follows the inspiring example of Christ. You will allow me to illustrate my words with a touching example from the Gospel of St. John. (8:3-11) "Now the Scribes and Pharisees brought a woman caught in adultery, and setting her in the midst, said to him: 'Master, this woman has just now been caught in adultery. And in the Law, Moses commanded us to stone such persons. What, therefore, dost thou say?'—And Jesus, stooping down, began to write with his finger on the ground. But when they continued asking him, he raised himself and said to them: 'Let him who is without sin among you be the first to cast a stone at her.' And again stooping down, he began to write on the ground. But hearing this they went away, one by one, beginning with the eldest. And Jesus remained alone, with the woman standing in the midst."

"And Jesus, raising himself, said to her: "Woman, where are they? Has no one condemned thee?' She said: 'No one, Lord.' Then Jesus said: 'Neither will I condemn thee.' "

We should interpret these words of the divine Savior in this manner: "I will not condemn you legally; I plead you free from the precepts of Moses' law; you shall not be stoned; so you may now go your way." But Jesus did not plead her free from the law of God: according to that law she doubtlessly had committed a sin. Now Jesus, in his infinite mercy absolved her from that sin; but, before dismissing her, he added this serious warning to his words: *"From now on sin no more."*

In this moving story we behold the divine Lawgiver setting an inspiring example to every lawyer who not only has the legal interest of his clients at heart, but who also wishes to promote their moral and mental well-being.

Christ is the example for every man or woman. He is also the stimulating example of the lawyer, because he is the greatest lawgiver of all times. When the House of Representatives was lately remodeled, twenty-three relief portraits in marble were placed around the walls, representing the great lawgivers in the history of mankind. Among them we miss Christ, and it is probably as well that he is not represented. For who is Moses or Solon or Hammurabi when compared with Jesus Christ? He stands out infinitely above all others, because he is the Eternal Lawgiver. They are the mouthpiece of the Law, Christ is the Law. They may be admired, Christ must be adored.

Reverence Through Biology

REV. HENRY E. WACHOWSKI, M.S.
Assistant Professor of Biology
The Catholic University of America

It may at first sight seem strange to include in this series of seminars designed for law students one on the relation of law to biology. The two seem to be disciplines rather widely separated one from the other, with hardly more than an accidental, passing relationship. If we stop to examine this relationship closely, however, we can, it seems to me, point out a fundamental problem unto which both law and biology converge, and in respect to which their aims and attitudes seem to be quite at odds.

It can hardly be denied that law both as a profession and as a science is rooted in the concept that man is rational, responsible, and therefore free and capable of being subject to law. In this sense the field of law might be called the bulwark of man's rationality—the bulwark of man's superiority to inanimate and lower animate creation;—a superiority that is one not only of degree but of kind. It must be quite clear that unless law is founded on such a concept it cannot long be more than simply a restraining pattern of action with no validity—it cannot long be more than a series of pragmatic regulations, to be used only in so far as they are pragmatic. The moment law ceases to be founded on notions of freedom, rationality, responsibility,—the moment its foundations cease to be transcendental, immutable values stemming from man's nature as a responsible, rational being composed of body and spiritual soul, then its nature must become relativistic—it must begin to use as its norm the greatest apparent immediate good for the greatest number. It then paradoxically becomes transformed from the protector of immutable human rights and values for all to a dispenser of comfort and license to the few. That this already has happened is evident for instance in the almost universal acceptance of legal divorce not only by the people generally, but even by those whose function it is to uphold law in the high sense which I have described for it above.

69

On precisely this point—on the point of whether there are immutable values founded in man's being which must be upheld—modern biology too has a great deal to say. To the uninitiated it may appear that the science of life, as it applies to man, might be able to shore up, to support the contention that man is special—that he is indeed a rational being, quite essentially different from lower creation. This does not seem to be so. The science of biology seems to be concerned with,—as a matter of fact takes for granted,—that man is nothing more than a complex of physical and chemical forces, operating in the same way, and according to the same laws, by which these forces are active in the inanimate world.

It may therefore be well to examine how this outlook grew in the science, and what its present implications are. At the time of Descartes physical sciences and mathematics had already succeeded in setting themselves up as fairly precise sciences by rigid adherence to a formula: Accept as true only what can be demonstrated with mathematical certainty. Descartes, surveying the chaos raging in philosophy, attempted to institute mathematical methods as a means of philosophical inquiry that would bring to that field the same admirable results it had already brought to physics and mathematics, and at the same time suggested that the application of the same methods to the study of living things would bring order and precision into the science of living things. It was he, in fact, who proposed that living things be analyzed as machines. Here it is that we have a parting of the ways; here it is that biology tacitly becomes a branch of physics and chemistry; here it is that the notion of no essential difference between living and non-living gained momentum.

Most significantly, it is here too that the foundation of modern biology on an essentially false philosophy was laid. This may seem a strange statement to make. It certainly is one with which many modern scientists will not agree; but it seems to me the facts are clear. The admission as valid biological knowledge of only those phenomena that can be demonstrated by measurement, with mathematical certainty, at once bases biology upon an epistemology from which the validity of the immeasurable is excluded. Notions such as those of purpose, final cause, are not epistemologic-

70

ally valid in such a system, and consequently cannot be acquired with certainty from a study of living things. It is often said that the role of science is a historical one—it consists of presenting to the philosopher merely a chronicle of natural phenomena for his analysis. This is hardly tenable from the standpoint of biology, for here, from the time of Descartes, the chronicle itself has been directed, pushed, weighted by a basic philosophical assumption: that only the measurable of living things is knowable.

This same attitude has persisted down to the present. Cartesianism has been replaced by Kantianism in science, and here too cause, purpose become simply maxims subjectively imparted to our conception of reality, so that they are once again stripped of objective validity. It is for this reason too that Darwin's theory enjoyed such immediate success. It seemed at first glance to offer a formula to which biological knowledge could be reduced very much akin to the successful formulae of physics. That this did not turn out to be true is really beside the point. The very search for such a formula indicates sufficiently the tie-up between biology and a false epistemology at the time of Darwin.

Even in the present the story is very much the same, although a certain restiveness can be detected. Biology has concerned itself with the breakdown of living things into their physical constituents. It has made of living things a mountain of chemical reactions. It could hardly do more, for it had assigned to itself the task of breaking living things, analyzing them, by the methods of physics. With such methods and such results, the biologist has almost unconsciously become convinced that there is nothing more than the physical and chemical in life. He has become certain that there is no essential difference between the living and the non-living; but simply that the former represents a more complex grade of the latter.

All the evidence accumulated by science therefore has been evidence interpreted against the transcendental, human values on which we described law to be built. As a result, responsibility, freedom, rationality have really become only conventions, subject to evolutionary change just as structure and form itself, and mutable in accordance with the needs of a particular time or place.

71

It must be quite evident that law, order, as we know them and as we need them for our service to God cannot long survive in such a medium. My plea therefore to the assembled law students—to any students for that matter—is twofold: First, interest yourself in the problems that science, and especially from my point of view biology as a science, faces. There are rumblings and minor revolutions already. Compton for instance finds it difficult to define science in terms of certainty; finds it difficult to fit biology into the accepted definition of natural science; the Organicists plead for less analysis and more synthesis in biology—they seek a study of whole organisms instead of parts of organisms. Cassirer in his *Problem of Knowledge* notes, after a lengthy discussion of vitalism and mechanism, that the science of biology is still to be defined, still to be established, if it is to be a science separate from physics. We, it seems to me, have been remiss in this field. We have permitted the sciences to go their own way, considering them to be indifferent disciplines. We have been content only occasionally to "disinfect" the sciences; our attitude has been a negative, defensive one. This attitude is hardly in keeping with our avowed purpose—"to restore all things in Christ". If we are to do this we must capture science too;—not by criticism and objection, but by producing capable, brilliant scientists whose epistemology is ours—a true, valid one;—one that admits the validity of other than knowledge gained by mathematical demonstration. This can be done only by an awakening of general interest among all of us in the fields of science, science which most of us have so far considered foreign and unimportant.

Secondly, and possible more directly, my recommendation to you is to "consider the lilies of the field". The best antidote against the removal of purpose, cause, the transcendentals, from our sphere of knowledge, and from your own field of law is to give even passing attention to the things which show these forth most clearly. In our specialized, highly practical "gadgeted" form of existence, we become, or tend to become, completely unaware of the marvels before us in the world. Consider the lilies of the field—the plants, the trees, the animals that cross your path; reflect on them—purpose, cause, an omnipotent Creator shine from every leaf, every petal, every insect, every living

72

thing. He is there for you to read and reach, if you but take the time to do so. Through biology there arises— reverence.

Literature, Art and Spirituality

HELMUTH ANTHONY HATZFELD, Ph.D.
Professor of Romance Languages and Literatures
The Catholic University of America

The discussion about the compatibility of Literature and Art with Spirituality goes throughout the Christian centuries, since the days of St. Justin and Tatian. Sometimes the same personalities during different epochs of their life change their view about this problem. Bossuet, one of the most refined prelates who edited himself the Greek and Latin classics for the Dauphin, who endeavored to produce rhetorically and literarily spotless works of French prose, one day joins the Jansenists in their categorical rejection of any dramatic art, even that of Corneille, Racine and Molière as endangering the soul. We do not quiet understand Bossuet's sudden change of view. What we would understand, however, without difficulty is this: that works of art which are not remote enough from the crude passions of life due to their lack of artistic perfection may produce not a catharsis but a shallow atmosphere of delectation. Such an atmosphere evidently is lethal to any spirituality, even the elementary one which struggles along the borderline of mortal and venial sin. What we would understand also is that the highest spirituality of asceticism and mysticism, having reached a detachment of the soul from everything that is not God, is not compatible with art, as it is not compatible with anything earthly and only indirectly linked to the Highest Good. But even here we must make distinctions. Artistically gifted saints used to give their theocentric contemplation an aesthetical form, Fra Angelico, for instance, by painting; St. John of the Cross by poetry.

The Church actually has always encouraged the arts of word, color and sound to join her in her worship. Therefore she has made out of her very heart—the Mass—a work of art by adding organic artistic accretions to its dramatic nucleus in the course of centuries. This is the proof that the Catholic Church, as different from the heterodox deviations from Christianity, holds that the arts are called up to the highest task of beautifying the *mysterium tremendum*.

It is with the help of the arts that the Church developed the ceremony of the Last Supper, including the Mystery of Calvary, into a symbolic drama. A real sacrifice, expressed in a symbolic manner, makes present the redeeming death of Our Saviour. It unites the partakers with the Divine Hero who pays for the guilt of others. The protagonist of this drama, the priest, impersonates Christ to such a degree that he speaks the words of consecration in the first person singular, peak of all Christian symbolism. The liturgical "staging" and the things meant by this performance coincide. A higher reality is expressed by signs, actually shown and seen. The supers in this supreme drama, the acolytes and the congregation provide like a Greek chorus for the ratification of the acts of the protagonist through their dialogue responses. They share mostly in the lyrical parts of the dramatic poem of the Mass, such as the Introit, the Gradual with its Alleluia-jubilation, the serious meditations of the Tract, the Offertory and the Communion verse while the protagonist stresses the dignity of *his* part, particularly by the rhetorical masterpieces of the Collects, the Secret, the Preface and the Postcommunion parts which he never would delegate to one of the acolytes as he would do with the less artistic although no less impressive and holy prose of the epistles and the gospels.

Nobody has seen better the character of the Mass as a dramatic, lyrical and rhetorical artefact than the famous French Romantic writer Chateaubriand who, in his work *Le génie du Christianisme* describes the literary art character of the Mass in the following way:

> Let us assume that the mass were an ancient ceremony, the prayers and descriptions of which were found in the secular poems of Horace or in certain Greek tragedies. How we would admire and praise that dialogue which opens the Christian sacrifice:
> —I will go unto the altar of God.
> —To God who giveth joy to my youth.
> This dialogue is a true lyrical poem between the priest and the catechumen: the first in the fullness of his life and experience sighs about the misery of man for which he is going to offer the sacrifice; the second, filled with hope and youth praises the victim by which he will be redeemed.
> Then follows the Confiteor, an admirable prayer for its morality. The priest implores the mercy of the Almighty for the people and for himself.

75

The dialogue begins again.

Then the offerer of the sacrifice mounts to the altar, bows and kisses with respect the stone which in ancient days hid the bones of the martyrs.

Remembrance of the catacombs.

In this moment the priest is seized by a divine fire: Like the prophet of Israel he intones the hymn sung by the angels above the cradle of the Savior and of which Ezechiel heard a part in the clouds.

The epistle follows the hymn. The friend of the Redeemer of the world, John, lets us know words full of sweetness, or the sublime Paul scoffing at Death, reveals the mysteries of God. Ready to read a section of the gospel the priest stops and implores the Eternal to purify his lips with the burning coal with which he touched the lips of Isaias. Then only the words of Jesus Christ are echoed in the assembly: there is the judgment of the adulterous woman, there is the Samaritan pouring balm into the wounds of the traveler, there are the little children blessed in their innocence.

What can the priest and the assembly do after having heard such words! They can't but declare that they believe firmly in the existence of God who has left such examples on Earth. Consequently the Creed is sung triumphantly.

Meanwhile the sacrificer prepares the host for himself, for the living, for the dead. He offers the chalice. He blesses the bread and the wine. He washes his hands:

"Take not away my soul, O God, with the wicked, nor my life with bloody men."

Remembrance of the persecutions.

Pray, my brethren.

The priest remains a moment in silence, then suddenly announcing things Eternal: *Per omnia saecula saeculorum,* he exclaims:

Lift up your hearts!
and a thousand voices answer:

We have lifted them up unto the Lord.

Then the preface is intoned upon the ancient recitative of the Greek tragedy: the Dominations, the Powers, the Virtues, the Angels and the Seraphim are invited to descend with the Great Victim and to repeat with the choir of the faithful the threefold *Sanctus* and Eternal Hosanna.

Finally the tremendous moment draws near: The canon, in which the eternal law has been written is opened. The consecration is accomplished by the very words of Jesus Christ.

At these words the Mystery receives its fulfillment. The Lamb descends in order to be sacrificed. . . .[1]

---

[1] Edition P. Garnier, vol. II, pp. 106-08.

Chateaubriand does not tell us, however, that this unique dramatic poem of the Mass is a theme with variations. Its variations are the different propers. And these again seem arranged together according to great leit-motifs. The *Laetare* Sunday[2] actually is a symphony in rose. Rose mitigating the violet of penance is not only the color of the vestments, but also the tenor of the prayer, which give to the still waiting catechumens and repenting and atoning Christians a first far off glimpse of Easter and hope. So in the Introit: *Gaudete qui in tristitia fuistis,* in the Collects: We are afflicted by sin: *affligimur,* but God can give us the grace to break the burden: *respiremus;* in the Epistle: We *seem* the sons of the bond-woman, but we *are* sons of the free woman; in the Gospel: Five barley loaves only, but of them Jesus *distribuit quantum volebat,* what a source of confidence!

But as we said above, the Collects, for instance, may be further analyzed as a true little artefact of rhetoric hinging on the two columns *affligimur* and *respiremus.* There is the *protasis* of guilt and penance leading to the slow and heavy *cursus tardus:*

> Concede quaesumus, omnipotens Deus,
> ut,
> qui ex merito *nostrae actionis affligimur,*

and the *apodosis* of consoling grace leading to the quick and joyful *cursus velox* with its literal breathing spell during the penitential fast:

> tuae gratiae *consolatione respirémus.*

The sinful will for evil deeds is contrasted with the consoling help of Grace in a veiling, mitigating, i.e. rose, not violet, chiastic, not roughly parallel antithesis:

> *ex merito* nostrae actionis
> tuae gratiae *consolatione;*

two *isocola* slightly opposed, as we just saw, by the proparaoxytonon *afflgimur* and the paroxytonon *respirémus.*[3] This is a truly Ciceronian architecture like (I say this for the jurists):

> Quousque tandem abutere, Catilina, patientia nostra.
> Quem ad finem sese effrenata iactabit audacia . . .

---

[2] This paper was read on Laetare Sunday 1951.

[3] Sr. M. Gonzaga Haessli, U.S.U., *Rhetoric in the Sunday Collects of the Roman Missal,* Cleveland: Ursuline College, 1930, p. 52-53.

While the modern English translations have give
strife of imitating the Latin rhythm correctly, the
of the sixteenth century did it almost to perfectio

> Graunte, we beseeche Thee, Almyhtye God,
> > that
> we which for oure evil dedes are worthely punishe
> by the comforte of thy grace may mercyfully be reléve

We certainly will subscribe to the judgment of Cardn.
Wiseman:

> Nothing can be more perfect in structure, more solid in
> substance, more elegant in conception, or more terse in
> diction, than the Collects, especially those of the Sundays
> . . . of Lent.

Such is verbal art used by the Church herself to foster
the spirituality of her faithful. We could continue now
with analyzing the Gregorian Chant as the most artistic or
rather artistically most appropriate music for the Divine
Service. But let us mention only the musical interpretation
of the Introit *Laetare* where, in the melody embracing
closely the text, appears a structure a little different, by its
inverse order, from the Collects. There is first the thesis of
a jubilant invitation to anticipate the joys of the Heavenly
Jerusalem (Santa Croce in *Gerusalemme* being, by the way,
the Station Church of the day), ardent, enthusiastic, im-
perative in zeal, full of awe. Then comes an antitheses of
tender, merciful, painful stress on *in tristitia fuistis*. This
shows that the Church as a Mother shares the penitential
sorrow of her Children exiled as yet from the Fatherland to
be reached through the Resurrection (Easter). A synthesis
of these two motives then is the consolation of the promises
of God.[5]

If this Introit is sung on one of the psalm tones in
churches without a choir, the whole beauty is destroyed.
If even the *Commune* is taken out of the Gregorian sphere,
a tremendous empathy on the part of the composer of new
interpreting musical patterns for the sacred texts is necessary to make the song compatible with the spirituality
which the Church wishes to express. The decision of the
Church in rejecting great musical artefacts as such, but

---

[4] *The Book of Common Prayer as issued in the year 1549,* Privately reproduced
for Mr. G. Moreton, Seal Chart near Sevenoaks, Kent, 1896, fol. CCCV.

[5] Dom L. Baron, *L'expression du chant Grégorien* (L'Abbaye Ste Anne de
Kergonan, Morbihan), 2 vols., 1947, vol. I, 272 ff.

artefacts not fitting in with the sacred texts, as incompatible with the *disciplina arcana* of the sanctuary and with the serving role of the sound when confronted with the Word of God, gives us an inkling that not every type of music is eligible for spirituality. When the jazz music in the twenties was first introduced in Germany (not in the churches, of course) the bishops launched a joint pastoral against it as a music stirring the passions and therefore incompatible with any spirituality, even that minimum which should belong to the status of every Christian. Now as far as the high spirituality of the liturgy is concerned the Church does not tolerate any *musica troppo molle* and bans the greatest names, Machaut, Ockeghem, Beethoven, Pergolese and more so Rameau, Rossini, Berlioz, Verdi, Mozart, Gounod from her liturgical drama.[6]

With this musical problem we have reached a first tension between art and spirituality. But we have also understood, that musical works of different styles—Mozart—Berlioz—Wagner—Debussy, excellent in themselves, may gradually become less compatible with spirituality also outside the Church, if these styles absorb rather the sensations than the psyche of the listener, if they arouse rather than appease, or appease in a sense of art for art's sake, as is the case with Wagner. There are cases where music, melodiousness, rhythmical insinuation become self sufficient, "divine".

Art, consciously serving the Divine by a spontaneous fusion with its sacred subject, practically has no limitation. But the forgetfulness of its destiny to serve leads it to assume the attitude of an usurped hegemony. The sculptural nudes on the tympanum of the Resurrection of the Cathedral of Bourges do not imperil at all the dignified character of the tremendous last judgment scene. The medieval sacred art was spontaneously governed by the spirit of the Church. since highly cultured bishops and abbots gave the artists the spiritual idea for their works, the many details of which were left to their inventive imagination. If the theme was. for instance, the Assumption of Our Lady, as is the case on one of the portals of Notre Dame of Paris, the artist was free in the choice of the two then current versions, the resurrection or the dormition. But he was supposed to present his sacred event on three levels according to the

---

[6] *See Motu proprio* of Pope Pius X, 1903.

technique of the figurative interpretation of Scripture. The event must have a bearing to the Old Testament, to the new dispensation and to the world to come. Thus we see on this Paris tympanum first a symbol of Mary: the Ark of the Convenant surrounded by kings and prophets of the Old Testament, ancestors and heralds of Mary. This is on the panel of the prefiguration. On the second panel is a wonderful interpretation of the *dormitio,* Christ with the apostles coming to guide his mother to Heaven; on the third panel there is Mary's coronation in Paradise.

To keep up the level of ecclesiastical art, the Church always depended on the combination of a creative, original spirituality and a creative art coming from an artistic genius. This constellation after the middle Ages has become rare. The worldly spirit of the Renaissance gave a terrific blow to medieval piety and it was said that nobody could ever really pray before a Madonna of Raphael. But the Spanish mystics again with their visions described, became a spiritual stimulation for the Spanish painters. When El Greco painted an Assumption he used the description of Santa Teresa's own ecstasy which she called the flight of the Spirit and of which she said that her soul was drawn out and upwards in a dilatation that she felt as though unknown powers were pushing her body, too, from below her feet. It is exactly this description that El Greco used to paint the most beautiful enraptured Virgin pushed and carried off by angels in a flight of an endless distance between Earth and Empyreum so that in her transfigured, beautiful, slim, actually dilated body the distance from feet to head seems immeasurable.

Thus we have an example of the highest spirituality, namely mysticism inspiring one of the greatest religious paintings. But we have even an example that a mystic who was a born poet could not help expressing his decisive mystical experiences in outstanding poems, that is, St. John of the Cross. A poem is symbolic by definition. This means that a highly delicate subject matter resists rational and philosophical language and urges for metaphorical expression, but so that this metaphorism as the closest analogy to mysterious experiences or happenings or relations includes likewise the lower reality from which the metaphor is taken and the higher reality for which it stands and which it tries to grasp. Now Saint John of the Cross was held a prisoner by the mitigated Calced Carmelites, who were opposed to his reform, in a terrible cell in which he was not even able to stand upright. Then it providentially happened that in this plight, ascetically so advantageous, he was graced by the spiritual marriage, and shortly after that he was lucky enough to escape from prison. Now in one of the most marvelous poems of Spanish literature, he combines the jubilant report of the happily overcome dark nights of his prison and of his soul; for he finally was shown that this dark night led to God, nay was God in a dark, not recognizable way, which became clear when the unitive illumination came and this apparent darkness proved light, quiet, liberty, bliss, union of the loving soul with the Beloved. This latter motif is linked to a third poetical layer hinting like an undercurrent at the mystical tradition of the Church and the Canticle of Canticles. Let us read some strophes of this poem:

Saint John of the Cross: *The Dark Night of the Soul:* (Translation Arthur Symons)

Flight: Upon an obscure night
Fevered with love in love's anxiety,
O hapless, happy plight!
I went, none seeing me,
Forth from my house where all things quiet be.[7]

Light in the Darkness: Blest night of wandering
In secret, where by none might I be spied,
Nor I see anything;
Without a light or guide,
Save that which in my heart burnt in my side.

Mysterious Goal: That light did lead me on,
More surely than the shining of noontide,
Where well I knew that One
Did for my coming bide;
Where he abode, might none but he abide.

Mysterious Wedding Feast: O night that didst lead thus,
O night more lovely than the dawn of light,
O night that broughtest us,
Lover to lover's sight,
Lover with loved in marriage of delight.

---

[7] Here is the first strophe of the Spanish original:
En una noche oscura
Con ansias en amores inflamada
¡Oh dichosa ventura!
Sali'sin ser notada
Estando ya mi casa sosegada.

81

Until now we have considered how the Church herself encouraged art in the direct service of God and how her artists and her saints used it to make liturgy beautiful and mysticism understandable.

The next point to be made clear is that art remains art, or as one said in the Middle Ages, God's grandchild, even if it serves God indirectly only, or as it is often subjectively intended, although objectively impossible, not at all. To bring this problem home as clearly as possible, I concentrate now on that part of art which constitutes my proper field of investigation, literature. I understand by art in the indirect service of God, literature as handled by epochs living in harmony with the Church and by art apparently not serving God at all, literature in a secularized world.

The first problem to be seen in this connection is that men of all ages, Christian and Non-Christian, write on three fundamental topics, love, country (state) or society, and nature either in poetry or in prose. But it may well be that the epochs living in harmony with the Church are more outspoken about a human ideal than those which we called secularized. The creative genius however *qua* genius, seems independent of the epoch and even of the objectively correct or erroneous "truths" which he presents as an expression of his subjective psychology in an aesthetic form.

Despite this theory, it would be foolish to conceal that in the course of history the two greatest Catholic centuries, the thirteenth crowning the Middle Ages, and the seventeenth consolidating the Counter-Reformation, have produced the two greatest literary works of the Occident, Dante's *Divina Commedia* and Cervantes' *Don Quijote*.

The reason why these works are so outstanding actually seems to be that they cannot help being spiritual, despite or together with their formal beauty, since for their Catholic authors every problem dealt with necessarily is a problem of faith. Dante's central concern is Love in its unbridgeable earthly-heavenly tension. His work of art, however, wants to be this poetical bridge which cannot be thrown in a philosophical way. Based on the fundamental truth that all love is one, he shows its growing into charity according to the elements of sacrifice and renunciation it assumes. In this lies the mystery of Beatrice.[8] She meets Dante as a

[8] Charles S. Singleton, *An Essay on the Vita Nuova*, Harvard: University Press, 1949.

beautiful girl walking through the streets of Florence and responds to his greeting her in such a gentle way that he feels she must love him and he enjoys the happiness of requited love. He jubilates about this mildest form of possession as far as a woman is concerned. But when he meets her again she refuses to requite his salutation and Dante realizes the unhappiness coming from unrequited love. He thinks relentlessly of her, her beauty and her gentle manners.

Greater sorrow and greater involuntary renunciation are in store for Dante, as Beatrice dies. And Dante's way out of his plight is treason to love; he tries to forget her by carousing with friends and "enjoying life" with women of a lower quality. But Beatrice, the pure, in Heaven, entreats God to warn Dante and to show him the truth on life and love in a vision which leads him through Hell, Purgatory and Heaven. In Heaven Beatrice, still the Florentine girl, despite her transfiguration enkindles the ancient love in Dante again, but this time love seen from the other side. And now Dante understands how he should have used his love experience: Beatrice by her behavior and by her premature death was destined to give him a lesson, that love, even of a woman, can quickly develop into charity, into the Love of God, into his very love that moves the sun and all the stars, if the element of egocentric desire is overcome by sacrifice. This lesson Dante first did not understand. Now in his vision of the Divina Commedia when the beautiful eyes of Beatrice only draw him upward and upward to bring him to the vision of God, he understands that this bliss wrapped in sacrifice began the very day in Dante's life when the young Beatrice, by not responding to his greeting, stepped aside to make room gradually for the love of God who is a jealous God and does not share in any other love but that which resolutely presents itself as a means of leading to him.

This subjective fiction coming so close to the heart of Christianity and intuitively found by this genuine Catholic poet conveys so many spiritual values to the reader that it was honored still six hundred years after the death of its poet by an encyclical of Benedict XVth who praised Dante Alighieri as the ideal Christian poet despite the fact that he populated his Hell with several of the popes who, as he believed, betrayed the Church which he made bold to love as much as they and despite the fact that in the greatest opposition to Saint Thomas he dreamt of a world empire to insure a relative, earthly happiness of the citizens, an empire whose head would not be the pope but the emperor. These features have been stressed here to show the enormous inner freedom of Dante in presenting also ecclesiastical aspects in his own way of interpreting the world which, shocking as they may appear to us modern Catholic weaklings, did not deviate in the slightest from his spiritual-artistic message.

The same problem repeats itself with the first modern novel from the beginning of the seventeenth century, the famous *Don Quijote* by the Spaniard Miguel de Cervantes Saavedra. Cervantes presents an idealistic knight, Don Quijote, who tries to arrange the best imaginable world according to his own ideas of justice, right and order. He is accompanied by a materialistic squire, the peasant Sancho Panza who, mainly interested in eating, drinking and money making, constantly tries to persuade his master to return to his home and abandon his ideal. The story which brings so many beatings and scoffings to Don Quijote seems just a funny story, but is full of spiritual depth and truth. Why does the idealistic knight undergo these constant defeats? Because he fights for subjective ideals which, anachronistic and outmoded, rather destroy a well established order instead of improving it. When he tries to oppose his lay activity to the contemplation of the monks as something greater and more important, even the materialistic Sancho teases him by the remark that he never saw knights and soldiers put on the altars. On his deathbed only, Don Quijote recognizes that stupid reading of adventure and love novels was responsible for all his mad idealism, which had been only in the service of his own egocentricity. Had he read books of piety instead, he says repenting, all these extravagancies would have been kept at bay. Consequently the *Don Quijote* is a Catholic novel driving home the very essence of the spiritual life, but so inconspicuously and in such an entertaining fashion, that representatives of all philosophies of life would swear Cervantes' Truth is also theirs.

Now we have reached a point where we are able to understand that poetry and a poetically conceived prose can convey to the reader spiritual values. But at the same time we have recognized, that the same works superficially looked at seemed not to contain anything of a spiritual message, but rather to offer ideas of revolt, romantic love, fanciful ideas and fun. Thus the great question arises, whether there are poetical schemes into which Catholic ideas can be pumped, or if there is such a thing as great and significant poetry which by dint of its essence must have recourse to certain symbolic forms of expression which spontaneously, even against the will of their authors, and necessarily convey a spiritual message to the reader. If the latter hypothesis holds true, then also poetry and prose in a secularized world, even from the hands of unbelievers, are bound to be a good thing and to bring a catharsis also to the Christian and Catholic reader in the same way as the inconspicuous, not dogmatically, but artistically presented Catholic truth affected favorably any kind of reader. How else to account for the praise of the classics in the educational programs of the Jesuits who expected from the Pagans: Homer, Virgil, Horace, Ovid, the best effects on their pupils.

Jacques Maritain seems right in thinking that certain sound ideas, imaginations, discoveries and observations have in common that they grasp reality. These grasps are in their synthesis of such an intuitive and artistic character that they never can be expressed in philosophical form but only in artefacts, mainly in poems. Poems, no matter who is their author, have such a power of catharsis on the reader that they make him re-experience—so to speak—in reading what the poet experienced in writing, a flash, a thrill, a purification on the aesthetical level. This is a secret, entirely in the natural sphere, of course, which no literary critic, philosopher or philologist could ever unseal. It is no mystery, it is nothing of a supernatural quality whatsoever, but it is a very great thing in the natural order. This catharsis in the natural order always will have the power to bring the reader a little closer to true spirituality, even in a secularized world. The main reason is that a great poem opens the interior eye to a particular reality which cannot be apprehended by our senses, which cannot be disclosed by speculation and which being of the natural order has

85

nothing to do with revelation but can, of course, be related to it by the Christian reader and his sensitive reaction to the artefact. This again has something to do with the suggestive power and the many-sidedness of any great poem.

Percy Bysshe Shelley (1792-1822), the young poet who was expelled from Oxford after having written the pamphlet *The necessity of atheism,* who abandoned his wife and tried to find in pantheism a substitute for religion, could not help as a poet creating literary artefacts which are true to the very bottom of their message and transcend any limited intention which Shelley might have had when writing them. Let us take his famous *Ode to the West Wind.* With a fascinating imagery the poem praises the stormy west wind of fall bringing with the dusk of the year sickness and death, but none the less preserving the seeds which a gentler spring wind will raise to a new life. The poet wishes to partake in this wonderful pattern of Nature where apparent destruction is preservation.

But the Christian reader sees in the poem without any difficulty the Eternal Easter Message, the Promise of Grace after Sin, Eternal Life after temporal Death and he cannot help thinking that the Destroyer and the Preserver Storm has the Pentecostal implication of the Holy Spirit, censor of the Soul, destroyer of the imperfections and preserver of the seed of contemplation to be developed into blossoms and fruit. The reader no less than the poet feels that he should be a lyre to be touched by such a Divine wind, breathing, blowing wherever it wishes. Let us experience this by reading a part of the poem:

Ode to the West Wind

O wild West Wind, thou breath of Autumn's being,
Thou, from whose unseen presence the leaves dead
Are driven, like ghosts from an enchanter fleeing,
Yellow, and black, and pale, and hectic red,
Pestilence-stricken multitudes: O thou
Who chariotest to their dark wintry bed
The winged seeds, where they lie cold and low,
Each like a corpse within its grave until
Thine azure sister of the Spring shall blow
Her clarion o'er the dreaming earth, and fill
 (Driving sweet buds like flocks to feed in air)
With living hues and odours plain and hill:
Wild Spirit, which art moving everywhere;
Destroyer and Preserver; Hear, oh, hear!

Make me thy lyre, ev'n as the forest is:
What if my leaves are falling like its own!
The tumult of thy mighty harmonies
Will take from both a deep autumnal tone

. . . .

Scatter, as from an unextinguished hearth
Ashes and sparks, my words among mankind!
Be through my lips to unawaken'd earth
The trumpet of a prophecy! O Wind,
If Winter comes, can Spring be far behind?

Controlling our impression at this point, we certainly will state: True poetry remains always poetry, i.e. a significant intense experience, phrased in symbolic, mythical, fictional, extraordinary evocative language which cannot be translated into logical, conceptual prose and which conveys instead a catharsis to the reader by which his empathy into a hidden, though natural reality or his sympathy with a fundamental aspect of being is aroused.[9]

This experience can even be made by such an extreme and hermetic poem as Stéphane Mallarmé's (1842-1898): *The Swan*, beginning with the line: "This virgin, beautiful and lively day." There is couched in mysterious language the story of the Swan who while he dreamt of impossible flights was caught by ice and frozen in his pond, not quite unwilling, since his dreams could not materialize anyway. The poetical quality of this poem lies in its pregnancy of symbolic meaning. Certainly, this swan is the poet who has the frightful awareness that writing down his poems means treason, abstention from doing so means keeping intact his most lofty imagination. The Virgin Swan intimates that the great realization of motherhood goes at the cost of the greater ideal of virginity. It means in a wider sense—and we come to the very heart of spirituality—that all the conquests of human activities are meaningless compared to the state of contemplation. It means that no theoretical ideal, the spiritual as little as the philosophical, artistic or biological can escape the Swan's dilemma that active realization and passive renunciation are incompatible, since the purity of the idea is contaminated by its contact with matter and never can materialize in an impeccable form. It is striking how thin is the wall that separates the aesthetic from the

---

[9] See definition of poetry by James Craig LaDrière in J. T. Shipley, *Dictionary of World Literature*, N. Y., 1943, p. 441.

moral and even metaphysical, nay, mystical implication in such a modern and secular product of the so called pure poetry. This is the poem:

The Swan

This virgin, beautiful and lively day
Will it tear with a stroke of its drunken wing
The hard, forgotten lake which haunts 'neath the frost
The transparent glacier of flights unflown!

A swan of past days recalls it is he
Magnificent but without hope
For not having sung the realm where to live
When sterile winter's ennui has shone forth.

All his neck will shake off this white agony
By space inflicted on the bird who denies it,
But not the horror of the soil where his plumage is caught.

Phantom that to this place his brightness assigns him,
He is stilled in the icy dream of contempt
Which clothes in his useless exile the Swan.[10]

While we thus may maintain that any type of true poetry is not only compatible with, but a stepping stone to spirituality, we would not make the same statement about the modern novel. The reason is obvious. It is not the usual theme of passion, sensuality, cruelty, sexual perversion which makes this novel dangerous, because all these topics could be expressed in a non-objectionable style. It is not the one or the other sensuous or crude or graphic passage which could be eliminated or replaced. It is rather the lack of transformation of the sinful life elements into the quiet realm of art which would make them lose their appeal to the sensations and direct them to the depth of the soul. It is the error of their authors who believe they can handle the human mystery as a problem from which they pretend to stand at a distance, while they are inescapably involved in it, and that they can treat in a fiction so close to life, human beings like things, i.e. without charity and from the impassive superman's viewpoint.

In other words, since, in general, the modern novel, for the reasons just mentioned, does not provide for a catharsis, but for an arousing of sensations and passions, it definitely leads away from an atmosphere compatible with spirituality and drives the reader more or less into the area of sin.

---

[10] Stéphane Mallarmé, *Poems,* translated by Roger Fry, London: Chatto and Windus, 1936, 171-173.

This is the reason why the technically most perfect novel of the nineteenth century, Gustave Flaubert's *Madame Bovary* is not a truly great work of art. As Charles Du Bos has seen very well, it is not the story of the doubly adulterous wife of a country doctor who poisons herself when debts and disgrace drive her into dispair that is objectionable, but the constant concentration of the interest on the physical and physiological, the body and the bodily movements, the dresses and the jewelry, the ideal-less boredom of an apparently meaningless life. Here human dignity is precisely violated even on the aesthetic level by a mask of impassiveness on the side of the author who makes bold to treat human beings as objects and thus degrades womanhood. Whoever closes this book will not feel elated but debased. The literary critic from his viewpoint cannot help joining the moralist in indicting this technically so overdone work as incompatible with spirituality.

This statement would not condemn, however, the realistic and naturalistic style as such. This style was used by Joris-Karl Huysmans and Léon Bloy whose Catholic books certainly would be compatible with spirituality, but these on their part are no real works of art, since the spiritual message they would have to offer lingers around narrative blocks in which they are literarily incapable of embodying it. A naturalistic novel, however, with deep spiritual elements as substance and organized in a readable, somewhat difficult and therefore dignified, and acceptable story was and is the rather recent achievement of Georges Bernanos and Graham Greene. Here the subject matter itself is based on an exact analysis of mystical phenomena, or the character of priesthood, or the vital essence of the sacraments for the faithful. Here, of course, some realistic or even stronger graphic elements never can detract mature readers from the cathartic atmosphere which the deep religious tension constantly maintains. The art consists here certainly in the apt, aesthetic fusion of truly religious problems with convincing plots. Still one could ask, however, if the catharsis here comes really from the artefact or simply from the problem, and if the good old Pagan Homer does not foster an atmosphere helpful to spirituality at least as much as the whole so called modern Catholic literature.

Thus, it seems, that spirituality as subject matter can only be an aesthetic modifier.

The curious fact remains that the restrictions of pastoral prudence almost coincide in these cases with strictly literary criticism which misses here restraint and measure. The pastoral critic would object, for instance, to Graham Greene's presenting a priest who is a debased drunkard, overlooking the fact that even this drunkard resists the temptation of not going to a dying person to whom he is called, since he is in danger of being arrested and killed by the communists. And with his death he becomes a witness of the greatness of the *character indelebilis.* The mysterious beauty of this fact has not been met aesthetically however in a satisfactory way. Pastoral prudence would recommend on the other hand Paul Claudel's constructed and invented dramatic episodes out of allegedly impeccable Catholic epochs where young girls give the charity kiss to the leper and become saints, or where a woman unhappy in her marriage is tempted to follow her lover, but is preserved by the Blessed Virgin to such a degree that again the lover and she herself become saints. The literary critic, however, will find that just these exceptional constructions are mere romanticism, because they are presented as normal in allegedly better times. They have melodramatic and operatic elements and precisely for this reason do not produce a pure catharsis but a sensational, though somewhat pious excitement. It is difficult to say, whether this type of literature, compatible with spirituality for its intricate spirit of sacrifice and love of God, is not too didactic, apologetic and demonstratively dogmatic in order to remain a work of art, even with the limitations inherent to the modern theatre. In Claudel's works there is too little of the burning actual problems to make them modern theatre and too much of the sensational to preserve them the dignity of timeless tragedy.

From all this we may conclude that the interrelations between literature, art and spirituality are extremely complex. No doubt that literature and art fulfill a great mission if they serve directly the beauty of the Divine Service, no doubt that any spiritual implications contribute to redeem even extreme forms of literature like the modern novel and theatre which under normal conditions contain too many troublesome and sensational life elements. But only a literature without any explicit tendency, e.g. "pure" poetry and classical epic and tragedy, by their very essence of art and its necessary symbolism, lead into realms of calm and purity which easily pave the way to true spirituality.

That is, I think, what Pope Pius XII meant when in his allocution to the Catholic artists in Castel-Gandolfo[11] he made the following remark:

"It is through art that the senses, far from weighing down the soul and nailing her to the soil, rather aid the soul like wings to be lifted from the fleeting meanness and shabbiness up to the eternal, to the true, to the beautiful, to the only true good, to the only center where union is accomplished, where unity is reached, to God."

It certainly is gratifying for modern criticism to have its interpretation of the Aristotelian catharsis and of the interrelation between art and spirituality shared and encouraged by the Supreme Pontiff.

---

[11] Text in French in *Osservatore Romano,* Sept. 6, 1950.

Nihil Obstat:
    WILLIAM H. RUSSELL
        Censor Deputatus

Imprimatur:
✝   PATRICK A. O'BOYLE
        Archbishop of Washington

August 9, 1951

CATHOLIC THEOLOGICAL UNION
BL65.L33W541951   C001
THE LAWYER LOOKS BEYOND THE LAW WASHING

3 0311 00006 5495